ASSESSING
Student Learning
and Development

T. DARY ERWIN

Foreword by Peter T. Ewell

ASSESSING
Student Learning
and Development

A Guide to the Principles, Goals, and Methods of Determining College Outcomes

Jossey-Bass Publishers

San Francisco • Oxford • 1991

ASSESSING STUDENT LEARNING AND DEVELOPMENT
*A Guide to the Principles, Goals, and Methods
of Determining College Outcomes*
  by T. Dary Erwin

Copyright © 1991 by: Jossey-Bass Inc., Publishers
                     350 Sansome Street
                     San Francisco, California 94104

                     Jossey-Bass Limited
                     Headington Hill Hall
                     Oxford OX3 0BW

Library of Congress Cataloging-in-Publication Data

Erwin, T. Dary, date.
    Assessing student learning and development : a guide to the
  principles, goals, and methods of determining college outcomes /
  T. Dary Erwin.
        p.   cm.—(The Jossey-Bass higher and adult education series)
    Includes bibliographical references and index.
    ISBN 1-55542-325-6
    1. Educational evaluation—United States.   2. Education,
  Higher—United States—Evaluation.   I. Title.   II. Series.
  LB2822.75.E78   1991
  378.73—dc20   90-22107
                                                           CIP

Manufactured in the United States of America

The paper in this book meets the guidelines for
permanence and durability of the Committee on
Production Guidelines for Book Longevity of the
Council on Library Resources.

JACKET DESIGN BY VICTOR ICHIOKA

FIRST EDITION

Code 9126

THE JOSSEY-BASS
Higher and Adult Education Series

CONTENTS

FOREWORD

Since assessment emerged as a national phenomenon in higher education some five years ago, its practice has been hampered by the lack of a book like this. True, there is no shortage in print of descriptive pieces, technical treatments, and unabashed polemics, but most of what has emerged as truly useful to campus practitioners amounts to a "shadow literature" of fading photocopies traded from hand to hand. As a result, many of us have gotten used to operating out of boxes, employing the usual combination of luck and accumulated experience to find and apply what we need. Given the multifaceted nature of assessment's development, this pattern is unlikely to change substantially. But what Dary Erwin has given us is invaluable: a place to start.

Doing this is not easy. Practicing assessment requires simultaneous familiarity with technical measurement practice, with the process and tactics of organizational change, and with the substance of what goes on inside college and university classrooms, counseling centers, and informal student gathering places. Writing about it effectively demands equal comfort with the language of all these activities. Setting a proper tone is critical to the success of such a volume.

One mistake often made by writers in the field is the overemphasis of measurement technology. Assessment practitioners remain, for better or worse, a band of "happy amateurs"; they are as

likely to be former English instructors as they are to be formally
trained in educational measurement. They need solid, often technical, information, but they need it in a form that they themselves can
understand; and, because they must work with teams of equally
nontechnical people throughout the campus, they need it in a form
that is communicable to others. A major feature of this volume's
appeal is that it discusses complex issues in a readable fashion.

But a second mistake can be equally objectionable: "dumb-
ing down" the discussion. Assessment practitioners throughout the
nation desperately need the straight stuff; "cookbooks" that gloss
over complex issues or intimate that there is a single "right" way
of doing things will not be sufficient. Erwin has admirably avoided
this pitfall as well. Readers will find a tough discussion, succinctly
covering most of the things they will need to know when they
actually do assessment. But they will also encounter an engaging
style, continually informed by accumulated wisdom and by plain
common sense.

Another daunting challenge in treating a controversial topic
is to avoid the false distinctions that often hamper effective communication. Assessment practice has been unusually subject to linguistic polarization of this kind. One such dichotomy is
methodological: a presumed opposition of "quantitative" and
"qualitative" techniques. In practice, these days, few of us actually
recognize this distinction, and in his discussions of such useful
"intermediate" techniques as judgment rating scales, Erwin has
artfully and appropriately avoided it. At the same time, he has
treated the conceptual basis of test construction in a way that is both
substantive and demystified. Such treatment is critical for campus
practitioners, because opposing campus factions often develop
around "measurement" issues, severely constraining the establishment of a meaningful institutional process. Regardless of their
background, assessment practitioners need to know the language
and central issues of measurement, lest the processes they design
have no more rigor than the ones they seek to supplant.

Equally debilitating can be distinctions between "academic
achievement" and "personal development." All too often in assessment, investigation of such attributes as self-confidence, tolerance
of diversity, and motivation are given second place behind purely

cognitive learning. Organizationally, these attributes are often automatically assigned to "student affairs," with little consideration by faculty that they, too, have a role in developing such qualities. Worse still, this dichotomy can allow important aspects of student attainment to fall through the cracks. Increasingly, for example, institutional statements of general education are focused not only on skills and content but also on the development of such "habits of mind" as intellectual tolerance and persistence. Such attributes are neither "cognitive" nor "affective" in the traditional lexicon, but legitimately span important aspects of undergraduate experience. Partly because he is one of the few assessment practitioners with substantial experience in both cognitive and affective development, Erwin has resisted the temptation to divide collegiate outcomes so conveniently. As a result, both arenas are fully covered, but their potential joint products are equally emphasized.

In sum, *Assessing Student Learning and Development* is a book from which many in a developing field can benefit. Experienced practitioners will find in a single place a cogent summary of most of the basic references on assessment; at the same time, they will undoubtedly encounter a few new tricks to add to their repertoire. For those new to the field—and often charged with establishing a campus-based program from the ground up—this volume should prove indispensable. Not only will it provide them with a plan of attack, but it should also give them an important leg up on the self-proclaimed "methodologists" (both for and against assessment) who abound on all campuses. For all of us, it is a book that was worth waiting for.

Boulder, Colorado   Peter T. Ewell
January 1991   *Senior Associate*
                                                    National Center for
                                    Higher Education Management Systems

PREFACE

Assessing Student Learning and Development is a primer designed for those who will collect, review, use, and submit evidence about the strengths and weaknesses of their educational programs—that is, their success or lack of success in nurturing student learning and development. More specifically, it is designed for higher education faculty, student affairs professionals, and administrators who are starting or continuing an assessment program, and also in part for state agency personnel and accreditation officials. It provides a comprehensive overview of the principles, purposes, practices, and uses of assessment. By now, most administrators and faculty in higher education know the need to document the worth of their programs and services, and some have even attempted to meet this need. The term *student outcome assessment* is most frequently used to refer to these activities; however, other phrases—such as planning and evaluation, institutional effectiveness, and studies of educational impact—abound. Higher education has always been open to scrutiny and even to self-evaluation; yet criticisms of the quality of our efforts have struck a chord with many groups. Legislators, coordinating boards, accreditation agencies, as well as individuals and organizations within higher education, have noted our lack of systematic evaluation programs. What evaluative measures we have used—such as grades, percent of faculty with doctorates, or number of library books—have been crit-

icized as inappropriate or as poor in quality. As we seek to respond
to these groups, we will need to ask how faculty, academic administrators, and student affairs professionals should conduct assessment activities. How do we state what is to be assessed? How should
we select from among existing measures? How do we design our
own methods and offer proof of their worth? How can we provide
evidence that our methods are sound? These challenges leave some
educators unsure of their response or confused as they grope
through the technicalities and complexities of assessment strategies.

This book summarizes the basic principles and philosophy
of student outcome assessment and focuses on several processes for
assessing students' learning and development. Because of this focus
on student learning and development, assessment in this book will
not encompass other and broader aspects of institutional and program evaluation, such as resource management and organizational
operations. Although it briefly describes the origins and evolution
of the assessment movement, this book does not make value judgments about this movement and its impact on institutions of higher
education.

Assessment is here to stay in some form, and this book is
intended for the educator who wishes to use information to improve
programs. And that is my premise about assessment: that information will be used at least in part in the educational decision-making
processes. Educators in higher education will conduct assessment
not because of state mandates but because it makes sense to consider
effectiveness data for future directions. The effective assessment program will reflect institutional differences but also will offer systematic, defensible evidence about how much the students learn and
how well they develop. The useful assessment program will also
examine how these levels of learning and development have been
obtained.

The focus here is on higher-order reasoning and affective
developmental outcomes of education, in addition to knowledge
outcomes. Most institutions purport to enhance this "holistic" perspective of education; yet many lack the expertise to assess their
effectiveness in these difficult-to-define areas. Another unique approach of this book is its emphasis on the quality of the assessment
information. A number of techniques are drawn from the field of

applied measurement to guide the faculty or staff member who must supply evidence of the precision and worth of a program's chosen assessment methods. Some faculty and staff have been conducting assessment activities for years, but their methods often lack refinement and could be improved. The term *methods* is used here and throughout the book to include a variety of sources of information, ranging from forced-choice tests to produced responses of performances, products, and processes to surveys.

Overview of the Contents

Presented in the book are a series of assessment steps, as indicated by the chapter headings, that are common to any assessment program. Whether the focus is on the major, on liberal studies, or on a student development program, the steps are essentially the same: defining educational objectives (Chapter Three); selecting and designing methods (Chapters Four and Five); collecting, analyzing, and using assessment information (Chapters Six, Seven, and Eight). Although each step may be carried out or conducted differently according to the nature or nuances of a particular educational program or service, the issues within these steps will need to be considered for an effective and functional assessment program.

Chapter One recounts the background and purposes of assessment in higher education, recaps past studies about college impact, and defines assessment. Chapter Two highlights several active institutional assessment programs around the country, describes the characteristics of their success, explains the need for planning the process with staff and students, and discusses several broad program applications. Chapter Three explains how to establish program objectives, so that educators will know what they want to assess before assessing it. Chapters Four and Five discuss the selection and design of assessment methods, including methods of ensuring the quality of the assessment information. Chapter Six describes various aspects of information collection and maintenance, including sampling issues and costs. Chapter Seven discusses techniques employed in the analysis and interpretation of assessment information. Chapter Eight emphasizes the need for using information for decision making; it focuses on factors that influence the use of results and on the ethics of assessment. The last chapter projects where assessment is heading and how it will be practiced in the future.

Acknowledgments

A number of colleagues and friends added tremendously to the writing of this book. Gary Hanson gave early support to my ideas about including student affairs units in the assessment process. Peter T. Ewell gave freely of his ideas in conversations and in unpublished papers that guided and reinforced notions I had. His emotional support uplifted me at times as well. Donald Farmer, Donald Lumsden, and an anonymous reviewer read the manuscript and quite appropriately pointed to the need for additional examples and for further elaboration. I value their judgment.

I am ever grateful to all my colleagues at James Madison University. I would particularly like to thank the following people for use of examples from their programs: Lynn Cameron, Mary Ann Chappell, Jean Dalton, Larry Foley, Alexander Gabbin, Reid Linn, Allen Lyndrup, Elizabeth Neatrour, William O'Meara, Gretchen Reynolds, Betsy Runyan, William Seigh, Kelly Showalter, Donna Sundre, Gerald Taylor, Richard Travis, and the student affairs directors. They not only allowed me to use examples from their programs, but also, and more important, they creatively demonstrated the value of assessment at this institution. My appreciation also goes to Ronald H. Carrier, Al Menard, Robert L. Scott, and Richard F. Whitman for their administrative support of JMU's assessment endeavors.

Other colleagues who have graciously shared their ideas and wisdom include Margaret Miller and Anne-Marie McCartan of the State Council for Higher Education in Virginia, Marcia Mentkowski of Alverno College, Michael Knight of Kean College, Patricia Hutchings of the American Association for Higher Education, and Stephen Richarde of Virginia Military Institute.

A special thanks to Gale Erlandson, higher and adult education editor at Jossey-Bass, for having faith in me and for providing the right amount of guidance. My appreciation also goes to the superb editing talents of Mary Manke of St. Louis University and Michele Schwartz and Dorothy Conway of Jossey-Bass. Thanks to

Ursula Delworth, my mentor, for planting many of these ideas as seeds years ago when we were together at the University of Iowa. Lastly, thanks to my mother, Barbara Erwin, and my in-laws, Arthur and Ann Warner, for their support.

Harrisonburg, Virginia   T. Dary Erwin
January 1991

THE AUTHOR

T. Dary Erwin is director of student assessment and associate professor of psychology at James Madison University. He received his B.S. degree (1972) in business administration and psychology and his M.S. degree (1975) in educational psychology, both from the University of Tennessee, Knoxville. He received his Ph.D. degree (1978) from The University of Iowa in student development and measurement.

Erwin is past recipient of the American College Personnel Association's Annuit Coeptis Award (1983) and of the American Association for Counseling and Development's Ralph F. Berdie Memorial Research Award (1985). He has served as chairman of the Measurement Services Association (1985–86) of the National Council on Management in Education.

Erwin was previously affiliated with Texas A&M University as associate director of measurement and research services and visiting professor of psychology.

His main research interest is in assessing the learning and development of college students. His articles on this subject have appeared in journals such as *Research in Higher Education,* the *Journal of College Student Development, Educational and Psychological Measurement,* and *NASPA Journal.*

To my family—
Patti, Zachary, Whitney, and Nathaniel

ASSESSING
Student Learning
and Development

ONE

The Emergence and Purposes of Outcome Assessment

What is student assessment in higher education in this country? Why does it exist? How long will it exist? What are the purposes of assessment? Who should be involved in assessment? And what is to be assessed? These are questions that many administrators, faculty, and staff in higher education are posing. Behind these questions about assessment lie deep-rooted concerns about the quality of higher education—concerns expressed especially by parents seeking greater value for their tuition dollars and by legislators, governors, and other government officials who want to know more about how well education is doing its job (Fiske, 1987). As early as 1984, then Virginia governor Charles Robb stated: "There is no question in my mind that the public is ready to pay for [college] quality. . . . But the public is not ready to pay for a mere continuation of the status quo, because the status quo is no longer good enough" (Cox, 1986). This powerful statement has been echoed by other governors. In fact, assessment has been a major topic for action at the recent National Governors' Association (NGA) conferences.

Basic Questions About Assessment

What Is the Assessment Movement? Outcome assessment is now mandated or soon will be mandated in a majority of states

1

(Blumenstyk, 1988). It is undertaken so that institutions can document students' progress in higher education—in other words, the "outcome" after their exposure to college. The National Governors' Association, as much as any group, gave life to this movement because of its shared vision that assessment is a catalyst for improving quality. In addition, the governors regard assessment as a broader process of defining more clearly the mission of each institution and encouraging the use of information for program improvement (Alexander, Clinton, and Kean, 1986).

Why Does Assessment Exist? Rossmann and El-Khawas (1987, pp. 4-5) report essentially three primary reasons for assessment: political, economic, and educational. To this list, a fourth could be added, the societal. Political forces perceived weaknesses in higher education (Finn, 1988) and began to question whether the vast expenditures in this area were justified. In the past, the value of higher education was automatically accepted; even in tight economic times, higher education fared well against other state needs. Today, finite state resources—coupled with competing demands for the same pool of funds—have caused governors and legislators to think about allocating greater amounts of funds to higher education. Faced with court-ordered mandates to improve prisons, mental health services, and other state services, state officials have shifted funds to these areas. In addition, the clamor for increased funding to grades K-12 has increased competition for funds within the broader context of education. Some members of the public believe that higher education has received its fair share in the past and that other sectors of education should now receive similar attention.

Perhaps the greatest reason for political support of assessment in higher education is that state officials want to understand where the money goes and how well it is being spent (Boulard, 1988; Ewell, 1984; Slaughter, 1985). For some years, the increase in numbers of students gave strong support to increased funding. Even in those times, educational administrators found funding for "brick and mortar" easier to acquire than that for educational programs. It is too simple and perhaps too harsh to criticize the legislator or college board member, typically a business person, who seeks to draw parallels between outputs from the business world and outputs in education. The benefits of education are complex, and educators must continue to describe and make new attempts to document these benefits. What do students gain from the college experience? What evidence of learning and development exists? From this perspective, assessment tries to define what education is, not just to measure how well we educate students.

Assessment also is needed in order to ensure a well-trained work force to support regional, state, and local economies (Rossmann and El-Khawas, 1987). Competition from other areas of the world and the need for greater technological sophistication are ample challenges to keeping our country economically viable. And education is the vehicle for training and preparation of individuals who in turn will use their talents in economically productive work. State planners now must view education as an economic investment (Ewell, 1989).

A third major reason for assessment comes from within higher education. Several major reports on higher education have concluded that institutions are not as effective as they could be and have pushed for curricular reforms. Perhaps the two most influential reports about assessment are *Involvement in Learning* (Study Group on the Conditions of Excellence in American Higher Education, National Institute of Education, 1984) and *Integrity in the College Curriculum* (Association for American Colleges, 1985). Heavily influenced by the ideas of Alexander Astin, the NIE report expressed a need for higher education to institute systematic programs to assess knowledge, skills, attitudes, and capacities from academic and cocurricular programs. The report particularly emphasized the assessment of student benefits from student involvement in the campus environment. The AAC report was more blunt in its call for improvement, referring to the absence of institutional accountability as "one of the most remarkable and scandalous aspects" of higher education (p. 33). The authors of this report proposed that faculties design and use appropriate techniques for measuring student progress. In another well-publicized report, the Southern Regional Education Board (1985) similarly warned that "the quality and meaning of undergraduate education [have] fallen to a point at which mere access has lost much of its value" (p. 9).

Overall, these reports question the quality of education, call for the assessment of student progress, challenge us to think broadly about the goals of education, and propose that we compare a student's academic achievement with that student's involvement on campus. Moreover, higher education's current assessment methods are suspect and lack credibility. For example, the number and quality of institutional resources are only indirect measures; and these measures, such as the amount of square footage or the percent of faculty with doctorates, may not be adequate benchmarks for students' learning and development. One would expect, however, that these measures of resources would be positively related to more direct measures of student learning and development. Other existing methods, such as grades, lack the credibility that they had in the past (Pollio and Humphreys, 1988). According to Williams, Tiller, Herring, and Scheiner (1988, p. 161), "the meaning and validity of grades vary considerably within academic programs, and too much between programs, for their widespread use as outcomes in institutional assessment." Goldman and Slaughter (1976) demonstrated the unreliability of grades, while the popular press plays up the "passing" of academically unqualified student athletes. Other education critics pose "Why can't Lee read?" questions.

From a more historical perspective, Resnick (1987) has compared the present period with another period in the history of higher education. In the years 1918–1928 and 1952–1975, higher education underwent two expansionary periods followed by calls for increased assessment. The number of students increased dramatically during these periods, and the types of students and programs also changed. In 1931, Weaver complained about "our overextravagant expansion of courses, our overgenerous extension of elective choices, and our overambitious attempt to accept all students and serve all masters" (p. 13). Varying entry-level skills, incoherence of general education, and competencies in the major field of study were under question. Then, as now, new assessment methods proliferated. "Comprehensive examinations" was the catch phrase in the 1920s and 1930s, whereas "assessment" reflects the current period (Resnick, 1987).

A fourth reason for assessment lies in the public's need to know more about higher education and what it offers. Citizens need to understand that a college degree represents something besides increased future earnings and technical training. They need to know not merely "What am I getting for my money?" but also "What is a liberal arts education?" Daughdrill (1988, p. A52), president of Rhodes College, states: "In academe, . . . there are no labeling laws, no lists of ingredients that distinguish one institution from another." Educators have wrongly assumed that the public understands the various meanings of education. Now is a time to define ourselves beyond the increased income that a college degree provides. The clear statement of what education is about, program by program and across all programs, contributes toward the public's understanding of our functions.

Resnick (1987) contends that the lack of public confidence in our colleges and universities must be countered through marketing, lobbying, standardized tests, and local assessment methods. The restoration of public confidence, in Resnick's view, is incumbent upon "recruitment of students, federal and state subsidies, foundation support, and even research contracts" (p. 10).

The lapses in public confidence about education have a longer history within the K–12 grades. Since the 1800s, the public has relied on standardized testing whenever its confidence in the quality or cost-effectiveness of its schools was shaken. In spite of any criticism leveled against standardized testing over the years, test usage has steadily increased. However, one noteworthy shift has occurred. That is, whereas tests have been used in the primary and secondary schools to monitor year-to-year learning growth, about two-thirds of the states have now mandated some form of minimum-competency testing that emphasizes exiting skills (Resnick, 1982, p. 191). The shift is therefore from student improvement to student accountability.

These four reasons for assessment will continue to receive the most media attention in the future. From the point of view of faculty or student affairs educators, however, perhaps the most important reason for assessment is to bring about curricular and program improvement. Faculty and student affairs staff will be most motivated to participate and to conduct studies of effectiveness because of the benefits for their programs and students.

How Long Will Assessment Last? Will assessment fade away as other issues in higher education have faded away? Trend followers in higher education can recall the issues of student access and equality during the 1960s and 1970s. The theme of the 1980s and 1990s is quality. The intense attention to assessment may not last; however, its effects will last because of the permanency of the actions being taken now.

First, assessment is likely to remain in some form because many policies and laws are currently in place. Such requirements are not often rolled back without much scrutiny. In addition to the various state initiatives, the federal government via the secretary of education (U.S. Department of Education, 1988; Vobejda, 1987) has declared that assessment of students will be a part of all accreditation association standards. This is a move to consider the quality of education rather than just the resources or inputs to the process. Inputs such as number of library books or background of instructors are important, but only within the context of how much students learn and develop.

Second, several states have already allocated monies to cover assessment costs or to reward favorable assessment results. For example, Virginia and Washington have infused permanent funds into institutional operating budgets to pay for tests, personnel, and other assessment-related expenses. In Colorado and Tennessee, funding incentives provide rewards for institutions to demonstrate increasing effectiveness, since assessment is tied to 2 percent and 5 percent (respectively) of these states' instructional budgets. These monies undoubtedly create an expectation that assessment should be ongoing.

One can expect assessment to remain for the simple purpose of accountability. The practice of accountability is commonplace in our world today, and it is realistic to expect its continuance rather than its deemphasis. Essentially, evaluation is built into most public programs, and higher education is one of the last areas to follow suit.

Requirements for assessment are still being shaped by states and other external agencies. To take no action or to lag in response to requests for assessment is to miss an opportunity to determine an institution's objectives and methods of evaluation. For the sake of institutional flexibility and academic freedom, higher education must participate in the formation of assessment guidelines. To ignore calls for evaluation is to allow other groups to choose methods of assessment, which are sure to influence educational goals. Besides the new accrediting requirements regarding assessment, both public and private institutions should pay heed to discussions about a proposed national standardized testing program. If a nationwide program is implemented, it is unlikely that the diversities in our institutions will be retained. As Kleiman and Faley (1985) claim, if professionals refrain from contributing, then nonprofessionals will go about evaluation unaided.

What Are the Purposes of Assessment at an Institution? Table 1 illustrates a framework for the purposes of assessment and the groups by which assessment results can be used. As the table shows, the two major purposes of evaluation are improvement (sometimes called formative evaluation) and accountability (often called summative evaluation). Feedback in a formative evaluation program is used to improve, or "form," education. Information collected in a summative evaluation program is used to make decisions about the overall contribution of the program or individual. Such decisions usually result in resource allocations or continuance at the institution. In formative education, the typical question is "How can we improve our programs/students/staff?" In summative evaluations, the questions are "Should we reward our students?" "Should we continue our programs?" "Should we promote staff?"

Table 1. Purposes of Evaluation.

Target of Evaluation	Improvement (Formative)	Accountability (Summative)
Programs	Users: academic departments and student affairs offices	Users: budget planners, decision makers
Students	Users: students (for growth)	Users: students (for upper-level standing or graduation)
Faculty/Staff	Users: faculty/staff (for development)	Users: makers of personnel decisions

The targets or objects of evaluation can be programs, students, or faculty/staff. Most of the assessment programs now in place focus on academic or student life programs; some assessment programs focus on or furnish feedback to the individual student. Currently, assessment does not usually include evaluation of individual faculty or student affairs staff. Besides the current lack of interest, other factors, such as student motivation, would have to enter into interpretations. At this time, there is no evidence to suggest that faculty or student affairs staff will become a target group for evaluation in the near future.

If an assessment program is to be successful, upper-level administrators must make clear what its purposes are. For example, if assessment information is used to determine whether students can continue to their junior year, as in the state of Florida, the purpose of assessment is to make summative evaluations of the students, and it is legally necessary to make this purpose very clear. If the assessment is conducted for program summative purposes, faculty need to be informed that programs will be rewarded according to demonstrated effectiveness. At most institutions, assessment programs are introduced for the purpose of program formative evaluation. In such assessments, information is used to strengthen program deficiencies; curricula might be revised, or a new student affairs program might be added. An increasingly common practice is to return assessment information to individual students. This information does not affect their academic standing but may be used for their personal growth. Students appreciate receiving such information, and the summary review serves as a learning experience in itself. In turn, increased student participation strengthens the assessment as well.

Although the various purposes and target groups for assessment have been presented as separate functions of assessment, in practice the dividing line among these cells is not always clear. Obviously, if the purpose of assessment is for accountability, the quality of the assessment information is extremely critical; the information must be able to withstand challenges concerning its precision and value. Assessment for formative evaluation purposes may not need to meet such stringent conditions of accuracy of measurement.

Who Should Be Involved in Assessment? Assessment has traditionally been directed toward the programs in academic affairs, dealing primarily with entering basic skills and knowledge in the major field of study. Do students have the basic skills, such as reading, writing, and mathematics, for effective functioning at the institution and in our society? What have students learned in their major field of study? These questions will continue to be a focus in assessment programs at most institutions. Consequently, offices of assessment have sprung up around the country (Ewell, 1984) to assist faculty in designing assessment methods tailored to their programs and in analyzing institution-wide assessment information.

Although student affairs has been involved in remediation programs, such as study skills groups, student affairs professionals have not been in the mainstream of assessment. That is, the programs of student affairs have not been a focus of most state mandates, in spite of the NIE report's emphasis on academic *and* cocurricular program assessment (Study Group on the Conditions of Excellence in American Higher Education, 1984). On the other hand, in a recent nationwide survey, Hyman, Jamison, Woodard, and Destinon (1988) found that as many student affairs divisions are now responsible for overall coordination of assessment activities as are academic affairs or institutional research divisions. So student affairs is involved organizationally in implementing assessment programs, but its programs and services often are not evaluated.

The role of student affairs in assessment also depends on the philosophy of its leaders and staff. Some student affairs professionals (Hanson, 1982; Lenning, 1980) view assessment as a mechanism to demonstrate their contribution toward their institution's educational mission. In the future, assessment can serve to motivate divisions of student affairs to define their philosophy more precisely. Will student affairs offer services solely to support the resource management functions of the institution, or will it offer services that enhance students' personal and social development? Resource management functions are day-to-day operational functions, such as the processing of applications or the registering of students, that do not directly affect students' education.

Most institutions do aim to develop the "whole student," beyond the transfer of vocational skills for employment. Mission statements in institutional catalogues commonly point to the development of students' character, citizenship, common values, and a composite of social and personal attributes. Do student affairs professionals contribute toward students' development in this area, or does academic affairs maintain sole responsibility, or are the activities coordinated for common developmental goals? Is education nurtured solely by the faculty in the classroom environment, or do students learn and develop outside their curricular experiences through living on campus, participating in extracurricular activities, or partaking of cocurricular activities such as plays, lectures, and community service events? Research evidence supports the importance of out-of-class activities that enhance the personal and social development of students (Pascarella and Terenzini, 1991). It follows that all areas of the campus environment should be assessed.

What Is to Be Assessed? As indicated in the preceding section, students are typically assessed in areas of learning and development through programs of basic skills, the undergraduate major, general education, and student affairs. *Learning objectives are cognitively oriented objectives*, including subject matter knowledge and skills. For instance, students can learn basic principles and theories of a discipline, or they can learn skills such as writing or computing. *Developmental objectives typically include cognitive and affective dimensions*, such as critical thinking, ethics, identity, and physical well-being. Lenning (1977) has reviewed and summarized a variety of educational taxonomies. Of course, the selection of educational objectives is unique to each institution and under the purview of administrators, faculty, and staff. Some critics say that higher education has enough to do just to define content knowledge and measure it. Others believe that higher education has a responsibility to educate for attitudes, leadership skills, and tolerance and trust toward other people. Astin (1988) agrees that these areas of development form the basis for "the implicit curriculum."

Learning and development objectives are assessed most commonly through basic skills programs; programs in the major, general education, and student development; and alumni feedback. Separate committees could be formed to guide or oversee each of these areas, with the exception of the major or student development programs, which should be decentralized to the academic departments or student affairs offices, respectively. The assessment committee delegates further definition of outcomes and recommendations for instruments to these committees. A basic skills committee typically determines the skills that students must have if they are to succeed at the institution. These skills are usually defined as reading, writing, and mathematics. Providing more specific definitions about the components within mathematics, for example, and determining which levels demonstrate proficiency are not simple tasks. In several states, such as New Jersey, Florida, Georgia, and Texas, basic skills outcomes and tests have been determined on a statewide level.

Assessment in the major is naturally handled within each academic department. Likewise, offices of student affairs determine their own educational outcomes and assessment methods.

General education assessment plans are usually incorporated within an ongoing curriculum committee, which most institutions have for oversight of liberal studies. General education may be conceptualized in a number of ways, but three common divisions are liberal studies knowledge, common skills across the curriculum, and developmental outcomes. Liberal studies knowledge would embrace interdisciplinary knowledge or skills in humanities, social science, and natural science. Curriculum skills might consist of higher levels of writing skills; and computing, speaking, numeric, listening, and library competencies. Developmental outcomes might entail cognitive development, critical thinking, ethical reasoning, maturity, and identity.

Beyond the learning and developmental objectives, an institution needs to consider what courses, curricula, programs, and services have impact on these objectives. It is not enough to measure learning and developmental objectives; a department, an office, and perhaps an institution must consider why certain objectives are or are not being met. What should be changed if expected outcomes are not met? In this book, the various influences of curricula, programs, and services are conceived as aspects of the campus environment. The components of the campus environment influence or should influence students in predicted ways, as stated in educational objectives. The most traditional way to enhance students' learning is through coursework. What other areas of students' involvement should be monitored and compared with the level of their learning and development? Astin (1984) has hypothesized that the greater the student's involvement in college, the more the student gains and learns. Involvement applies to student effort and diversity of experiences in and outside of the classroom.

At least three assumptions are made here about learning and development as applied to higher education: (1) Learning and development can be enhanced and accelerated through education. (2) Changes in learning and development are relatively permanent. (3) The goals of education can be comprehensive, including more than just acquisition of knowledge. Education in this context applies not only to classroom experiences but also to other influences, such as programs and services within the campus environment. Maturation also influences learning and development, as do other off-campus experiences in the student's life. Part of the goal of assessment is to discover and document those on-campus attributes that influence students' learning and development.

Studies About College Impact

Studies about the impact of college on students predate current assessment interests. Excellent reviews of such studies have been provided by Jacob (1957), Feldman and Newcomb (1969), Bowen (1977), Pascarella (1987b), and Pascarella and Terenzini (1991). On the whole, these past studies have been empirically based and focused more on affective outcomes than on cognitive ones. For example, Jacob concluded in his initial review that seniors have "more homogeneity and greater consistency of values" (p. 4) than freshmen, but these changes were attributable to the socialization of college, not to the impact of a curriculum. Feldman and Newcomb were more specific in their probing and found the following "changes . . . characteristic of nearly all American colleges": " 'open-mindedness' (reflected by declining authoritarianism, dogmatism, and prejudice), decreasing conservatism in regard to public issues, and growing sensitivity to aesthetic and 'inner' experiences. In addition, a majority of studies show declining commitment to religion, increases in intellectual interests and capacities, and increases in independence, dominance, and confidence as well as in readiness to express impulses" (p. 48).

This line of research has given rise to a variety of taxonomies, models, and theories about how students develop during college. Lenning (1977) has compiled perhaps the most comprehensive collection of possible "outcomes" from college. In his review of over eighty schemes for classifying goals of higher education, he places the various schemes in the following categories: intellectual development; emotional, cultural, and social development; physical and psychomotor development; society and individuals; and a general category. More complex models have been proposed in student development by Chickering (1969) and Heath (1968, 1977); in broader theories of human development, models have been constructed by Belenky, Clinchy, Goldberger, and Tarule (1986), Kohlberg (1964), Loevinger (1976), and Perry (1970). Some of these models are discussed in Chapter Three.

Until recently, college impact studies, along with the taxonomies and theories of development based on these studies, have received little attention except from scholars conducting research in these areas. Very little transfer occurred from research findings to practical applications in higher education policy (Ewell, 1988b). Although Rodgers (1990), for example, has applied theories of student development to program planning, assessment has generally not served as a guide for program planning or evaluation.

Also missing from these college impact studies is a focus on the learning and cognitive aspects of the undergraduate experience. Subject matter learning has been left to faculty in their respective disciplines. The subject areas of the Graduate Record Examination offered some information; but this examination was completed by graduate school–bound students, and the results were not generalizable to undergraduates as a group. Other isolated tests, such as the National Teacher Examinations, were used for screening purposes but not for a comprehensive program structure. Even students' perceptions about teaching were studied (Braskamp, Brandenburg, and Ory, 1984), but that evidence was seen as an indirect measure of student learning.

Background and Definitions of Assessment

The term *assessment* existed in at least two other contexts before it became popular in higher education. In business, industrial psychologists adapted the concept of "assessment center" that the armed services had used to make personnel decisions during World War II. For example, military personnel were assessed for crucial positions such as pilots and secret agents (Thornton and Byham, 1982). Similarly, assessment centers were applied in business to screen, select, classify, and place employees. The first industrial application occurred at American Telephone and Telegraph Company (Bray, 1964, 1982; Marchese, 1985). Although assessment center suggests a place, the assessment center concept, initially detailed by Murray (1938), actually entails multiple techniques of paper-and-pencil tests and situational performance tests. A paper-and-pencil test might include a personality scale; in a situational performance test, observations are made of people performing under simulated work conditions. For example, the Educational Testing Service first created the in-basket technique (Frederiksen, Saunders, and Wand, 1957) to simulate the way that a manager or an executive deals with an "in-basket" filled with memos and directives. More recently, Development Dimensions, Inc., under the auspices of the American Assembly of Collegiate Schools of Business (1987), has created assessment exercises in which this in-basket approach is used to measure a variety of personal characteristics for business students.

In psychology and educational levels K–12, assessment typically meant individual student appraisal (that is, "psychometric testing") as an adjunct of counseling and therapy. For instance, information about an individual student's abilities, interests, and personality was used for personal growth, for placement into advanced courses, or for selection into special educational programs (Salvia and Ysseldyke, 1978). "Psychometric testing refers to the systematic study of individual differences among people along specified traits or dimensions. . . . Psychological assessment . . . is more generally a process of problem solving" (Maloney and Ward, 1976, p. 38). In this context, assessment usually meant a one-to-one relationship between assessor and student, with the focus on the student rather than a program. Assessment also signified clinical expertise rather than test administration functions. That is, assessment embraced a more comprehensive approach to information gathering, whereas testing suggested a more narrow and specific focus. Just as in business, assessment in education included paper-and-pencil measures and situational performance measures, such as individual intelligence tests that elicited open-ended responses during a systematic interview.

Education, at the kindergarten through twelfth-grade levels, broke out of this individual student–centered approach to assessment when, in 1955, the advent of the optical scanning machine enabled assessors to gather data mechanically for efficient scoring of large numbers of students (Baker, 1971). Moreover, the need to examine the abilities of entire student bodies emerged when watershed events such as *Sputnik* fueled the demand for better schools in this country. With this emphasis on group scores, assessment often seemed synonymous with testing. To professional psychologists, however, assessment remained a more comprehensive and individualized activity.

Out of this background, the term *assessment* has proliferated in higher education. In a sense, its meaning today depends on one's role as state official, accreditor, administrator, faculty member, student affairs staff, or student. It also carries varying definitions and interpretations in the state-by-state guidelines (Boyer, Ewell, Finney, and Mingle, 1987). To the general public, however, assessment is linked inextricably with teaching, so that assessment is viewed as intrinsic to education itself (Ewell, 1989).

Definitions

In this book, assessment is defined as the systematic basis for making inferences about the learning and development of students. More specifically, assessment is the process of defining, selecting, designing, collecting, analyzing, interpreting, and using information to increase students' learning and development. It includes discussions about what should be assessed and how information will be used, not just the hands-on testing of students (Marchese, 1987).

A variety of people should be involved in these discussions, most of which are not technical. There is a side of assessment, called *measurement*, that is highly technical and quantitative; but assessment and measurement are not entirely the same. In fact, institutions that view assessment as just a process *or* as just a set of technical tasks either will risk basing their decisions on faulty information or will have difficulty implementing any results.

Measurement is the assignment of numbers to objects (such as an essay or a laboratory project), events (such as an artistic performance), or observations (for instance, of a student's response to a test question) according to some rule (Allen and Yen, 1979). In the assessment process, interpretive information is based on the quantitative results obtained through measurement. What type of quantification to apply to student behavior is the concern of measurement. Measurement also enables one to make determinations about the quality of the assessment information collected—most notably, its preciseness and its accuracy.

The field of *evaluation* offers another perspective on the definition of assessment. Although the terms *assessment* and *evaluation* sometimes are used interchangeably, evaluation is generally used in a broader context, which might encompass institutional effectiveness beyond students' learning and development. For example, an institution might evaluate the effectiveness of its campus parking system. Parking is certainly key to the functioning of the institution, but it is not directly related to the institution's educational mission. The focus of such an evaluation is not on the student but on the efficiency of a campus's parking operations. Educational evaluation, in the broad sense of organizational decision making, is closely allied with Stufflebeam and his colleagues' (1971) approach, which specifies the following process: (1) Delineate information needs for decision makers. (2) Collect supporting information. (3) Provide information to decision makers. Tyler's (1950) view of evaluation is probably more closely akin to the practice of assessment in this country today: (1) State behavioral goals. (2) Design measurement instruments. (3) Collect data. (4) Interpret findings. (5) Make recommendations. For Tyler, evaluation is the "process of determining to what extent the educational objectives are actually being realized" (p. 69).

Models such as Stufflebeam's (1973) decision-making model have been touted as alternatives to the more goal-oriented approach in this book. House (1980) reviews these other models, and it may be useful for some readers to pursue such models further. The goal-oriented approach has become the more practiced approach because the National Governors' Association, in its report on education, has emphasized the importance of defining institutional mission and intended outcomes (Alexander, Clinton, and Kean, 1986).

A joint committee representing twelve organizations has defined evaluation as "the systematic investigation of the worth or merit of some object" (Joint Committee on Standards for Educational Evaluation, 1981, p. 12). It is this judgmental aspect of "worth or merit" that is disturbing to some people; thus, in some contexts, the term *assessment* becomes a euphemism for evaluation of students' learning and development. Nevertheless, in a state such as Tennessee, assessment and evaluation are highly similar because of the accountability focus.

In the past, assessment was associated with individuals, and evaluation with groups and programs; however, this distinction does not hold in higher education. For Lenning (1980), assessment is the link between measurement and evaluation. Measurement offers no value judgment of merit or worth, whereas evaluation does. As Murphy (1975) and the Alverno College Faculty (1985) remind us, "assess" means to "assist the judge" or "sit beside." Of course, who makes judgments in the assessment process is often unclear. Is it the state or the institution? Within the institution, is it the administration or the faculty and the student affairs staff? These issues will be discussed in greater detail in Chapters Seven and Eight.

Lenning's (1980) definition of assessment reads: "Assessment refers to gathering data, transforming data so that they can be interpreted, applying analytical techniques, and analyzing data in terms of alternative hypotheses and explanations" (p. 234). To this description, this book adds other steps to each end of that process—specifically, "determining what is to be assessed" at the beginning and "implementing the results" at the end.

Assessment, measurement, and evaluation have in common the tools of testing; but these terms are not synonymous with testing. In particular, assessment is a more encompassing process than testing. Here, the terms *test, instrument, rating scale,* and *assessment method* all refer to a measuring method, procedure, or device "requiring responses from students that are capable of being scored in a consistent manner" (Roid, 1979, p. 67). Messick (1989, p. 5) offers a comparable definition: a "test score [is a] means of observing or documenting consistent behaviors or attributes." In practice, a test is a series of items or questions written to represent the content domain of interest. These test items can also be conceived as self-presentations or external observations of behavior, not just mutiple-choice questions. Glaser and Klaus (1963) view tests as techniques "for evoking particular behaviors by means of specifically designed stimulus situations" (p. 450). A test, then, is a tool, whereas assessment is a process for solving problems and answering questions. The solutions and answers will be based on information from tests and scales; however, tests are not the end point but part of the process of assessment (Maloney and Ward, 1976).

"Assessment of learning and development" is the phrase used in new office titles and on new state assessment legislation. But what does "learning and development" mean? Houston (1976), Mikulas (1974), and Strom, Bernard, and Strom (1987) have provided formal and precise explanations. More briefly, *learning* generally refers to the "acquisition of knowledge or behavior" as a result of one's experiences (Mayer, 1982, p. 1040) or, in this setting, one's education. *Development* is typically synonymous with growth or progressive changes in the person. These changes can be cognitive or affective or both. For example, the outcome "tolerance" suggests both a cognitive component (a flexibility of thinking) and an affective component (an openness of feeling or emotion).

Learning and development overlap, particularly in the cognitive realm, because both include reasoning and more sophisticated levels of thinking. In fact, developmental psychologists subdivide developmental changes into tasks or stages. Each task or stage represents a more complex level of human functioning, with different ways of thinking or feeling at each level. Some definitions (for example, Oerter, 1972) suggest that learning can encompass development or that development can include learning. In any event, both terms usually include most of the possible goals of education.

The next chapter will explore a range of programs that have evolved from the diverse purposes and interpretations of assessment. It will also draw some general conclusions about the kinds of consensus that must be built before any program is successful.

TWO

Building an Effective Assessment Program

Over the years, the practice of assessment has evolved into a wide variety of applications. In this chapter, several of the most active institutional programs are highlighted, and their common characteristics are pointed out. Assessment is both an art and a science, and the process of building consensus is just as important as the technical concerns. This process is explained from the perspective of staff and students. The last part of the chapter looks at some of the benefits and changes that can be expected from a successful assessment program.

Pioneering Institutional Assessment Programs

Faculty and staff are often guided in their own assessment implementation endeavors by reviewing the work of other model programs. This section briefly features some influential and innovative assessment programs of the 1970s and 1980s.

Ewell (1985) highlights three institutions as being in the "first wave" of schools that made early commitments to establish assessment programs and became national pioneers. These schools are Alverno College; the University of Tennessee, Knoxville; and Northeast Missouri State University.

At Alverno College, "assessment-as-learning" is a centerpiece of the curriculum, which defines eight broad abilities: communication, analysis, problem solving, valuing, social interaction, responsibility for the global environment, effective citizenship, and aesthetic response (Alverno College Faculty, 1985, 1989; Loacker, Cromwell, and O'Brien, 1986). Because Alverno emphasizes a developmental approach to educating students, each ability is defined via six pedagogical levels in general education and the major professional areas. Students, faculty, and trained assessors from the Milwaukee business and professional community assess knowledge and abilities by applying descriptive behavioral criteria to a student's performance on faculty-designed instruments. Each student receives feedback, and also self-assesses. An assessment center—based on industry's model—supports out-of-class assessments. The abilities, the instruments, and the assessment process itself are validated against internal and external standards by Alverno's Office of Research and Evaluation (Mentkowski and Loacker, 1985). Through a variety of strategies, the Office of Research and Evaluation examines the short- and long-term impact, value, validity, and effectiveness of Alverno's educational approaches and programs for students, alumni, and other college constituencies (Mentkowski, 1988). With its pioneering program, Alverno has advanced the concept of assessment for student formative purposes.

Northeast Missouri State University underwent a metamorphosis from normal school to university, and assessment became a catalyst in this change. Perhaps Northeast Missouri is most widely known for its advocacy of Astin's (1974, 1977, 1982) value-added approach, in which an entering student's scores are compared with the same student's scores at a later period, such as graduation. Northeast Missouri also focused on norm-referenced interpretations, when available, and concentrated on maintaining a comprehensive data base. Information centered around demographic variables, standardized achievement and ability data, and attitudinal data. In addition to improving faculty morale and student satisfaction, assessment was a successful tool for Northeast Missouri to document its improvement to its public constituents (McClain and Krueger, 1985).

The University of Tennessee, Knoxville (UTK) launched its assessment program in the early 1980s under the coordination of Trudy Banta (1985). In response to financial inducements outlined by the state of Tennessee (Tennessee Higher Education Commission, 1983), UTK targeted its assessment efforts "in achievement in general education, achievement in the major, and opinions concerning the quality of academic programs and services" (Banta, 1985, p. 20). Like Alverno College, UTK staffed its Center for Assessment Research and Development not only to coordinate organizational endeavors but also to provide technical assistance in the design and analyses of assessment data.

In the mid-1980s, a "second wave" of institutions followed with active assessment programs (Ewell, 1987; Hutchings, 1987). These institutions included King's College in Pennsylvania, Kean College of New Jersey, James Madison University in Virginia, Miami-Dade Community College, Mt. Hood Community College, South Dakota State University, Ball State University, Ohio University, Rhode Island College, Clayton State College in Georgia, and the State University of New York College at Plattsburgh. Although each institution contributed uniquely in its practices, only the first three will be described here because of space limitations. Other reviews about unique contributions to assessment exist (see, for instance, Paskow, 1988).

King's, Kean, and James Madison underwent broad-based and comprehensive reviews of their educational practices. Discussions were not limited to assessment but included various aspects of the curriculum and student development. For example, King's College adopted a core curriculum in three liberal learning areas: (1) transferable skills of liberal learning; (2) knowledge, traditional disciplines, and interdisciplinary perspectives; and (3) responsible believing and acting. The eight transferable skills are (1) critical thinking, (2) creative thinking and problem solving, (3) writing, (4) oral communication, (5) quantitative analysis, (6) computer literacy, (7) library and information technology, and (8) values awareness (Farmer, 1988). These skills formed the basis of the college's core curriculum and of courses within each major program. Each undergraduate major program delineated competencies by educational level pertaining to these eight skills. For instance, a freshman computer competency for English majors reads, "The student will be able to use word processing software to prepare, edit, revise, and present early and final drafts of assigned papers."

Kean College (1986) has also focused on assessment in general education, the major, and student development. A separate state-run basic skills testing program was already in place. In general education, locally designed assessment methods focus on content and critical-thinking skills. For example, essay tests are given in composition, emergence of the modern world, intellectual and cultural traditions, inquiry and research, and landmarks of world literature. A multiple-choice test and an essay test are given in "Science and Technology in the Modern World" (Gray, 1989, p. 5). The focus at Kean is primarily on locally designed assessment methods, with the faculty carrying the responsibilities for design and interpretation. Like King's College and James Madison University, Kean College stresses skills, subject matter knowledge, and human and professional values in its assessment program.

James Madison University assesses in the major, in general education, and in student affairs and also uses its assessment program to identify high-risk students. General education is defined through skills across the curriculum, such as writing; through liberal studies knowledge; and through student development, such as cognitive, moral, and psychosocial development. Like the University of Tennessee, Knoxville, James Madison University established a separate office of student assessment to assist faculty and student affairs staff in the design and analysis of assessment data.

These programs are successful for several reasons. First, they have upper-level administrative support. A president or a vice president for academic affairs issued public statements about the importance of assessment at the institution. Second, the people responsible for these programs had the flexibility, at least in the initial stages, to design their own goals and methods of assessment. Third, the assessment emphasizes program improvement first and accountability second. Fourth, although most of these institutions have an office of assessment or rely on outside consultants, the academic and student affairs departments also are involved in the assessment efforts.

Innovative programs also have been developed at other institutions. For example, at Baldwin-Wallace College, in Berea, Ohio, an Appraisal Center was established along the lines of the industrial "assessment center" concept. In the institution's Office of Career

Services, the Appraisal Center provides feedback to students about "interpersonal and oral communication, decision making, leadership, and clarity of career goals." Students are assessed in simulated employment interviews, in role-playing situations, and in unstructured group exercises (Rea, 1987, pp. 21–22).

Probably the individual who has rendered and sustained the most exemplary assessment studies in student affairs today is Gary R. Hanson at the University of Texas. He consults with all student affairs departments about program effectiveness. Individual studies range from minority student retention to profiles of student subgroups.

Characteristics of Successful Assessment Programs

Assessment programs that produce positive, cooperative changes have certain characteristics in common. Some of the characteristics or principles discussed here have been described by Miller (1989) and Ewell (1988a, 1988b, 1989); others come from personal experience.

First, successful assessment programs involve many people in the assessment process. The heaviest involvement, of course, is from the faculty, who assume responsibility for the definition and assessment of their programs. Although there is less day-to-day involvement on the part of administrators, their inclusion in the process is essential at certain points. They must make clear that assessment is primarily for program improvement, not for faculty evaluation. They must exercise leadership and not seek to defend the institution's good reputation by denying that any problems exist.

Second, there are clear, assessable educational goals and objectives. These objectives are reflected in the curricula for the undergraduate majors and for the general education programs. For instance, vague goals of "cultural and historical background" in general education are replaced by more specific statements about what students should know about culture and history. For successful student affairs assessment programs, clear developmental objectives are specified, and the educational mission of each office is well understood by secretaries and professionals alike.

Third, other constituent groups have been brought into the   *3*
process. A variety of persons outside the participating department— for instance, currently enrolled students, former students, employers, or colleagues at other institutions—have contributed ideas and comments about the program objectives, assessment methods, and, in some cases, interpretations.

Fourth, the data collected are meaningful, valuable, and ac-   *4*
curate. Methods are selected or designed with care, and evidence is available for reliability and validity. Generally, multiple methods are used.

Fifth, the data are analyzed and not just tallied for com-   *5*
pliance purposes. Efforts are made to study what the data mean for the program—what is working well and what needs improving. Programs that merely comply have poor survey return rates, no expectations about students' performances, and no concern about why students performed better or worse.

Last, a system is established for distributing and implement-   *6*
ing assessment results, so that the results are available to the people who can use them. Moreover, administrators make sure that the results are used. The entire assessment process is integrated into the planning and evaluation process of the institution, and the assessment information and reports support other review efforts, such as accreditation studies or annual program reviews. In contrast, in unsuccessful programs, assessment information is distributed or understood by no one except the report writer.

Building Commitment from Faculty and Staff

As previously discussed, assessment is a process that should include as many participants as the institutional scope dictates. These groups include upper-level administrators, faculty, student affairs staff, and students. The inclusion of diverse groups of people from around the campus conveys a sense of openness to campus groups and encourages wide-scale participation. The lack of cooperation from any of these groups can greatly weaken any institutional assessment program.

The initial tone of assessment is set by the administration, which can clearly communicate the purpose of assessment at the institution. Administrators should make clear how assessment results will and will not be used. The role and scope of assessment must also be delineated, so that no misconception exists about state requirements or about the amount of involvement by campus groups such as the division of student affairs. On some campuses, key administrators, such as a provost or a vice president of academic affairs, may speak against assessment. Such positions usually place the institution at odds with a state coordinating board when the same energy could be used to shape state assessment policy or to secure funds needed for its implementation.

The support of the faculty is vital to an administration that wants to institute a successful assessment program. Given time and opportunity to establish program objectives and assessment methods within a department, faculty generally plan and design a very workable system for valuable feedback. However, it takes only a few disgruntled faculty to sabotage or hinder assessment-planning efforts. The honest questioning of assessment is a natural and expected activity when assessment is introduced in an academic department, but failure to come to a consensus on departmental objectives or continual haggling over methods hurts everyone involved. Highly vocal faculty who oppose assessment without reason can poison not only other faculty's enthusiasm but also students' thinking about an assessment program. Therefore, faculty and staff reactions to assessment should be anticipated and taken into account in the early promotion of an assessment effort. Although it is difficult to categorize faculty reactions completely, they probably will include the following five stages: discovery, questioning, resistance, participation, and commitment.

Because many faculty members and student affairs staff are not familiar with assessment, or do not perceive it as something that affects them, the initial phase of assessment is one of *discovery* and introduction. Sometimes it is helpful to refer them to articles on the subject, so that they can gain a better sense of the background of assessment. Student affairs staff often find assessment easier to understand because many of them have had some training in testing in their graduate programs. Regardless of training or background, the national scope of assessment is generally a surprise to most people at the local level in higher education.

After the scope of assessment has been introduced to faculty and staff, institutions can anticipate a period of *questioning* about assessment. Why are we doing assessment? What is the problem? What have I done wrong? Is this a plot to eliminate my program? How will the results be used? Is this another waste of my time? Although most faculty readily understand the reasons for student outcome assessment, and although some of them have been assessing their students on a regular basis for years, many faculty express concern that participation in assessment will take time away from their other duties. Other faculty feel threatened by assessment and react with fear and occasionally with hostility. Student affairs staff may have similar reactions because of possible changes in their jobs: "How will it change what I do?" Most student affairs staff question the form assessment will take because there are fewer models to study in their area.

After a short period of questioning, many faculty move into a period of *resistance* against the assessment process: "My program goals cannot be expressed in writing." "What we are trying to accomplish cannot be assessed while they are students." "Don't lock me into a static list of goals." "You cannot measure what we do with students." "Employers hire our graduates, so what other proof do you need?" In particular, there will be resistance when outside "forces" request a statement about program goals and purposes. Faculty correctly should question the purposes of assessment at their institution. How will the results be used? Faculty should also be clear about what their role is in the process. For example, can faculty choose their own assessment methods? Who will analyze and interpret the results? It helps to have faculty consult with their colleagues in Tennessee, Missouri, or other states where assessment activities have been commonplace for a few years, and to know that they are not alone in this venture.

Resistance comes from student affairs staff who are service oriented, as opposed to developmentally or educationally oriented. Some student affairs staff do not agree philosophically that their roles should contribute directly toward students' education. They believe that their roles are ancillary to the educational process. Other student affairs staff believe that their profession does contribute toward students' education but are not sure how students benefit. These individuals feel apprehensive about learning a new approach.

Most resistance goes away when faculty begin to participate in assessment, and it is important for as many faculty as is convenient to be involved. At this stage, the stage of *participation,* faculty have to accomplish a task to meet a deadline. Some may still feel that participation or involvement is being "forced" on them, and they may say resignedly, "If we have to do it, let's do it." In student affairs staff, the compliance stage is more positive, because assessment is discerned as an opportunity to demonstrate their worth in educating students. Often perceived as a minor part of the educational process, student affairs staff are more willing to participate in assessment, although they often are uncertain how to proceed.

The last stage, *commitment,* generally comes after about a year's involvement. After faculty have discussed goals of their program, collected assessment information, and examined the results, they begin to see benefits in the assessment process. There are still questions and doubts, yet the value of assessment through program improvements is usually perceived.

Gaining Cooperation from Students

Useful assessment information can be collected only if students take the assessment activities seriously. If students do not put forth a reasonable effort, the information can underestimate their learning and misrepresent their development.

A number of strategies can be employed for eliciting students' cooperation in assessment. But even when these strategies are used, it takes time to build cooperation or to make assessment an expected part of the "student culture." The initial assessment activities are especially difficult because there is no precedent or past history of assessment, so that the first students wonder why no one before them had to participate in these activities. As assessment becomes more commonplace and more publicity is generated about assessment, it becomes a more expected activity. This process of "building assessment into the student culture" should be carefully planned, so as to increase the likelihood of student acceptance. The following guidelines can help educators anticipate students' reactions and elicit their cooperation.

Do Not Surprise Students. Perhaps the worst approach to take is to spring a test on graduating seniors, who have had no prior announcement of the activity and do not know its purpose. "Report to Room 100 at 1:30 P.M. for senior testing." Students will rebel loudly or resist quietly by marking responses at random on a test. Students, like most of us, do not enjoy such surprises. Therefore, early and repeated announcements should be made about any required assessment activity, including its purpose and the students' role.

Explain the Purpose and Expectations of Assessment. Just like faculty, students want to know "Is it required?" "If I don't do it, what will happen?" If assessment results are to be used for accountability or for summative evaluation, the consequences must be spelled out clearly for students. If assessment information is to be used for program feedback, educators can enlist the help of students as partners in the process, to obtain useful information for the benefit of the institution.

Although mechanisms for communicating the purposes of assessment will vary in the different institutions, the following techniques have proved helpful. Assessment requirements should appear in the institutional catalogue, in a statement that carefully lists the times for assessment and explains how the results will affect students' academic standing. A sample insert might read:

Student Outcome Assessment Consent Form

In order to comply with the guidelines of the State Coordinating Board on Higher Education and the Southern Association of Colleges and Schools, Local College requires a series of student outcome assessments, particularly at the beginning of the freshman year and at the end of the sophomore and senior years. I understand that these assessments are a required part of my education experience, will be kept confidential, and will not affect my academic standing. Rather, they will be used along with other students' test scores to identify relative strengths and weaknesses in the educational program, so that Local College can continually improve. I agree to participate in such assessments when requested over the course of my undergraduate period.

The purposes of assessment can be explained to new students and their parents during orientation periods. Although the students probably will not remember specific information about assessment from orientation, the mere mention of assessment helps prepare them for later assessment activities. When institutions administer placement tests or general education measures at entry, the link between the activity and its purposes is easier to make. In any event, the inclusion of an assessment announcement during orientation conveys the importance of the assessment process at this institution.

Working through an institution's advising system is another way to ensure that students understand the purpose of assessment. For instance, advisers can regularly discuss assessment activities in conjunction with students' program-planning efforts. This link can become a vitally important bond if the adviser feeds assessment information back to the student.

Include Students on Assessment-Planning Committees. Each institution will establish a number of assessment-related committees to deal with the role, definition, and use of results. Placing at least one student on each committee will ensure student input and create another link between students and staff. These students can be encouraged to report back to other students the nature of assessment.

Use Existing Student Groups for Publicity. Educators can ask the editors of the student newspaper for their help in communicating the importance of assessment and of students' cooperation. To generate interest and to focus attention on assessment, feature articles can be written just prior to a major assessment activity. For example, if an institution administers a general education instrument to second-semester sophomores, a feature article describing who is to be tested and how the information has been or will be used would reinforce the purpose of the testing. This outreach approach usually produces more accurate information for students and occasionally positive endorsement in editorials.

A collective meeting with the major student leaders on campus also helps to elicit student cooperation and understanding. Most campuses have a student leadership council, composed of students representing student government, multicultural student alliances, residential halls, sororities and fraternities, student activity or programming boards, commuters, and other special-interest groups. Educators can bring these leaders together to explain briefly the assessment movement and mandate and the purpose of the assessment. These leaders should then be encouraged to pass along this information to other students in their organizations. Obviously, this approach will reach only a fraction of the students, but this process should be viewed as part of a multistep effort for reaching the students.

Consult Student Affairs Staff. Student affairs staff work with students daily and can often serve as other avenues for reaching them. For example, dormitory advisers can help in encouraging students to participate at designated times. Even if a division of student affairs is not directly involved in developmental assessment, it can assist in building assessment into the student life or culture.

Explain What's in It for Them. Although most institutions focus on program evaluation, some students do not visualize a direct benefit of assessment for their education unless they receive individual student feedback. Consequently, institutions that focus only on summarizing information might add another purpose of assessment: reporting assessment results to individual students for their own learning and development. Alverno College, for example, uses assessment information as an agent in the learning process for individual students. Receiving feedback about one's strengths and weaknesses reinforces abilities and suggests areas for improvement. Such feedback also gives the student a vested interest in the assessment program.

Applying Assessment Information

When assessment results indicate that action should be taken, what kinds of changes can be made? How should the information be used? In general, the assessment process can elicit changes in (1) curriculum requirements, (2) curriculum content or student service programs, and (3) methods of instruction or service delivery.

Making Changes in Curriculum Requirements. In most academic departments and student affairs units, changes will occur in course requirements or student development program offerings just as a result of the first step of establishing program objectives. The discussions of what is to be accomplished or what is to be assessed usually produce changes in what is required of or offered to students. Typically, more structure is built into program requirements. For example, curricula for the major may be tightened. Most commonly, discussions about how to define a liberally educated person produce changes in the distribution or core curriculum requirements of a liberal studies program. In student affairs, some services may be dropped or new ones added. As one residence life director stated, "We realized we needed to give students more responsibility in some areas, and dropped some support services." Perhaps a new workshop for returning women might be offered to meet a developmental objective of "making educational and career plans."

Studies about who takes what courses can lend some guidance for requirement changes. For example, one academic department found that enrollment in certain elective courses in the major was associated with much higher outcome scores. A course that was previously an option was therefore made a specific major requirement. If an "enhancing leadership" workshop is associated with higher development scores, the workshop might be offered more frequently. If an internship or field experience is linked with positive outcome results, additional external experiences can be made available or required. If attendance at a fine-arts series is associated with higher scores on an arts or aesthetics test, perhaps attendance should be required.

Making Changes in Curriculum Content or Student Services. Requirements may be kept the same, but the content within courses might change. Deficiencies may be discovered in some sub-fields of a discipline through scores that were lower than faculty expectations or lower than those of students at peer institutions. Such problems are commonly found in the area of writing. If writing skills are less than expected, perhaps more writing assignments should be incorporated into the curriculum. In student affairs, it might be found that residence life programming based on Chickering's student development model produced higher developmental scores than a traditional residential programming style based on a regulatory model.

If deficiencies are found or new models are shown to be more effective, faculty and staff development workshops should perhaps be provided in these areas. If computing skills of students are deficient, perhaps faculty skills are outdated. Deficiencies may also suggest that no one is available to teach in the area of weakness. A social work department hired a new person in social research methods after alumni pointed out a program weakness that was verified by an assessment of current undergraduates. A liberal studies program found students weak in multicultural issues and therefore hired faculty to teach modules in black, Asian, and Hispanic studies.

Occasionally, deficiencies are found in academic service courses. For instance, a physics department found deficiencies in certain mathematical skills. Physics and mathematics faculty met to reconstruct the content of the mathematics service courses required for a physics major.

Making Changes in Methods of Instruction or Service Delivery. Do study-abroad courses enhance students' learning or development more than on-campus courses do? Is the use of particular software packages or computer-assisted instructional modules associated with higher learning scores? When assignment of roommates in dorms is based on developmental information, is the dropout rate reduced and student development enhanced? If students' working experiences are associated with greater development in areas such as independence, should additional financial aid money be redistributed from loans to work-study programs?

Of course, institutions will find other ways to use assessment results, and other examples will abound (Light, Singer, and Willett, 1990). Possible applications are limited only by the objectives and needs of the institution.

Conclusion

Now that an overview of assessment has been presented, the remaining chapters will explore the principles, purposes, and procedures that both fueled and evolved with the expanding presence of assessment on all types of campuses. These aspects of assessment are presented as a series of steps to follow in implementing any assessment approach. These steps of assessment are, or should be, common to any assessment program, regardless of focus. The objectives, the assessment methods, and the organizational units may differ from institution to institution; however, each of the steps must be addressed at some time for an effective assessment program. The order of the steps presented here is important, too, because each step builds upon the previous step. Of course, an institution will sometimes need to go back and revise selected components of the process. Part of the value of assessment is that it provides institutions with information that they can use to make improvements.

THREE

Establishing Objectives
for Outcome Assessment

An effective assessment program begins by establishing program objectives. One must know what is to be assessed before one knows how to assess it. This chapter gives examples of different types of educational program objectives, explains how to construct objectives, and describes components of the campus environment that can help students reach those objectives. As Williams, Tiller, Herring, and Scheiner (1988) posit: "We need to know more about what and how our students learn and what role we play in the process, in order to know what to teach and how to teach it" (p. 164).

Most college catalogues present institutional goals, purposes, or mission in the form of broad concepts, such as character, citizenship, or cultural appreciation. Because these goals are global and often vague, it is necessary also to state objectives. Objectives are typically expressed in a list or series of statements indicating what the department, program, or office is trying to accomplish with the student. What, specifically, is to be taught to the student? What specific skills should the student know? How is the student expected to develop personally and socially as a result of a specific program? Outcomes are the achieved results or the actual consequences of what the students demonstrated or accomplished (Dressel, 1961; Gardiner, 1989). Objectives may also be thought of as intended outcomes, and the assessment results as the actual outcomes.

Departments in academic and student affairs should state program objectives before they choose assessment methods. This step of writing down specific program objectives may take longer than some faculty and student affairs staff expect. Often, our terms are implied and are not clear to someone who is not in the discipline; moreover, consensus within a department may be difficult to reach. Typically, this objective-setting exercise produces much discussion, which often spills over into the curriculum and services offered. For example, Hutchings (1990) asks what benefits students in an English course gain from reading and discussing a paper called "Lost in the Funhouse" or what benefits history majors gain from working at the local historical society. In fact, many programs are changed during this objective-setting step before any assessment information is collected.

For various reasons, some faculty and staff do not like the terms *goals* and *objectives*. Therefore, other terms—such as *indicators, competencies,* or *outputs*—occasionally are substituted for *objectives*. Some academic disciplines prefer their own language to describe aspects of what is called here the assessment process. Language of the assessment process here is not limited to objectives but also encompasses terms covered later in the book about methodologies. Regardless of the terms used, it is important that what is to be assessed be stated as clearly and specifically as possible before any assessment method is planned or data are collected. The purposes are to decide what is to be assessed and to have educators in a given department discuss their common intentions in teaching or delivering student services.

Some writers (for example, Geis, 1970) advocate that instructional objectives be stated as active behaviors, such as procedural steps in displaying a skill (for performance objectives) or specific products or changes in other people (for consequence objectives). Other writers (Mager, 1962) believe that objectives should be stated as behaviors *and* as standards; for example, "The student can state at least three reasons why the United States entered the Civil War." However, the assessment process can become bogged down if these rules are followed to the letter. Instead, a department should simply make an initial attempt to state what its programs are about in as specific terms as is practical and politically viable within a consensus of its faculty and staff. Furthermore, program objectives are dynamic because of changing knowledge, and program intent will be changed as assessment information is used as feedback.

Occasionally, a department or an institution will skip this step of establishing objectives and will proceed directly to selecting a test marketed by a testing organization. The test is then administered without serious consideration of its appropriateness to a program. If scores are lower than expected, the natural reaction of some faculty members is "to teach to the test" in order to improve students' scores. That is, some faculty members, either consciously or unconsciously, will alter the content of their teaching to ensure that they are teaching material covered in the proprietary test. The focus of the test has then become the focus of the program's objectives. The shift in program focus is unintentional but real. Objectives established prior to actual assessment of students can guide the selection of assessment methods. The program objectives must drive the assessment methods and instruments, not the other way around. Methods for examining proprietary tests to determine whether questions relate to what is actually being taught are discussed in the next chapter.

Types of Objectives

Subject Matter Objectives. The most straightforward objectives are knowledge or subject matter objectives. That is, students are expected to learn the vocabulary, principles, and theories associated with the discipline. In the field of accounting, for example, the student is expected to understand the application of fundamental accounting theory to nonprofit entities. More specifically, the student must be able to perform the following procedures (as specified by Gabbin and Erwin, 1990):

1. Classify government activities into one of the five categories recommended by the National Council on Government Accounting—that is, general funds, special revenue funds, capital projects funds, debt service funds, and special assessment funds.
2. Use "modified accrual accounting" to recognize expenditures and revenues of a state or locality.

In speech pathology and audiology, the student is expected to understand communication processes and strategies (Runyan and Krivsky, 1988). Specifically:

1. The student will phonemically transcribe all standard English phonemes in nonsense syllables, words, and connected speech.
2. The student will identify the major phonemic and phonetic variants of Eastern American, Appalachian English, Southern American, and Black English dialects.
3. The student will identify the anatomy and physiology of the speech mechanism, audio-vestibular system, and relevant neurological structures.

In theatre, the student is expected to know the basic elements in at least one area of technical theatre. Areas of possible exploration include lighting, set design and construction, costuming, makeup, properties, and sound (James Madison University theatre faculty). Specifically:

1. The student should know how to construct a soft covered flat, a standard ridged platform, and a simple step unit.
2. The student should know the difference between the various theatre spaces: proscenium, thrust, arena, etc.
3. The student should know the basic principles of rigged flying scenery.
4. The student should know the basic principles of scenic, lighting, and costume design.
5. The student should know how to research properties.
6. The student should know the duties of a production team.
7. The student should know how to operate power and hand tools safely.
8. The student should know basic safety procedures of a scene shop and theatre space.
9. The student should know the basic materials commonly used in theatre production.

Each of the objectives above is stated clearly, singly, and factually. Subject matter objectives, being the most directly stated, should probably be formulated first, before more complex objectives are delineated in areas such as cognitive and affective development.

Developmental Objectives. Developmental objectives serve as purposes of general education, the major, and divisions of student affairs. Developmental objectives—which concern the ways in which people express their mode of thinking and feeling—are commonly referred to as *cognitive* or *affective,* although the two are often interrelated and difficult to separate. Cognitive developmental objectives are descriptions of higher-order thinking skills, including critical-thinking skills. Affective developmental objectives refer to attitudinal, personal, and social dimensions nurtured through the college experience. Some educators have referred to inclusion of affective objectives as "developing the whole student."

Developmental objectives are probably more permanent and lasting in their impact on students than are subject matter objectives. Ask a person what are the most important benefits from college, and invariably some type of developmental objective will be expressed. Subject matter objectives are often forgotten; developmental objectives serve the student through life and career changes.

Three popular conceptual approaches are offered here as illustrations for understanding and applying cognitive developmental objectives. These approaches are Bloom's (1956) taxonomy of cognitive objectives; Miller, Williams, and Haladyna's (1978) instructional intent categories; and Perry's (1970) scheme of intellectual and ethical development.

Bloom and his committee defined six levels in which cognitively related objectives may be categorized: knowledge, comprehension, application, analysis, synthesis, and evaluation. These areas are briefly described below; for each area, examples of the use of key words in stating an objective and of a test plan from the discipline of American government (Whitney, 1970, p. 3) are provided.

1. **Knowledge:** lowest-level category, involves the remembering or recall of specifics.
    Key words: To define, recall, recognize.
    Sample test plan: Define "balance of power" in the United States government.

2. **Comprehension:** a low level of understanding, including acts of translating, interpreting, and extrapolation. Ideas are not related to one another.
    Key words: To translate, transform, state in one's own words.
    Sample test plan: Can properly qualify statements of presidential authority.

3. **Application:** the use of abstractions to perform in a new situation.
    Key words: To generalize, relate, organize, classify.
    Sample test plan: Can use principles defining congressional responsibility to prescribe treatment of current legislation.

4. **Analysis:** breaking down the elements of a situation and clarifying the rankings or relations among the elements.
    Key words: To distinguish, detect, discriminate, contrast.
    Sample test plan: Can identify differing motives of interest groups, as expressed in bicameral legislature, three branches of government, and other constitutional provisions.

5. **Synthesis:** combining elements to constitute a new pattern or structure.
    Key words: To produce, modify, restructure, originate, derive.
    Sample test plan: Can develop constitutional grounds for a recent Supreme Court decision.

6. **Evaluation:** using a set of criteria or standards as a basis for making judgments about an issue.
    Key words: To evaluate, judge, appraise, rate, weigh.
    Sample test plan: Can develop criteria that special-interest groups might use to judge the desirability of certain constitutional provisions.

Miller, Williams, and Haladyna (1978; see also Roid and Haladyna, 1982) outlined a six-category system for classifying objectives and test questions or rating items: reiteration, summarization, illustration, prediction, evaluation, and application. *Reiteration* is essentially the recall or recognition of material from its original form. Examples of verbs within this category are: recall, list, name, locate, restate. *Summarization* includes reporting the essence of the material beyond simple recall. Examples of this category include: condense, abbreviate, paraphrase, translate, and describe. _Illustration_ prompts the student to use or recognize new examples for the given concept or principle. Sample phrases for this category include: provide an example, illustrate, construct, identify. _Prediction_ is the anticipation of an unencountered situation or unknown event. In this category, the student employs a rule or scheme to make this prediction. Descriptive verbs are: predict, estimate, anticipate, guess, expect, and extrapolate. _Evaluation_ "involves the employment of a criterion to render a judgment, decision, or selection." It requires analysis and a decision. Descriptive verbs include: decide, rank, judge, and evaluate. _Application_ is a problem-solving category where the student is requested, given an initial state, "to arrange conditions necessary to achieve" a desired effect. Descriptive verbs include: apply, formulate, plan, devise (Miller, Williams, and Haladyna, 1978, pp. 23–26; Williams and Haladyna, 1982, pp. 165–166).

In another scheme of cognitive functioning, Perry (1970) posited nine positions or stages, from lowest to highest. Erwin (1983b) collapsed these nine positions into three stages and added a fourth and higher stage. The lowest stage is _dualism,_ or the capacity to view the world only in concrete and simple terms. A dualistic person usually views issues as something to be agreed or disagreed with, ignoring any reasons behind these opinions. Dualistic persons are rigid, inflexible, authoritarian, and structured in their thinking. The next stage is _relativism,_ in which an individual begins to perceive alternative or relative points of view. Recognizing differing perspectives or viewpoints, the person compares and contrasts alternatives. The third stage is _commitment,_ the process of selecting among the reasoned alternatives. A person at this level has advanced beyond relativism, or recognition of alternatives, and is making commitments. This person has selected beliefs according to reasoned judgment. The highest stage is _empathy,_ or the making of commitments while realizing the effect of those decisions on other people. It is an awareness that decisions are made within the context of society and that decision making affects other people (Perry, 1970; Erwin, 1983b).

Dualistic objectives are usually basic knowledge objectives, such as the terms, introductory principles, and theories of a discipline. The relativistic person sees beyond basic facts that are presented as given and begins to make comparisons among theories and principles. The committed person reasons and reflects about the alternative, often contrasting, theories in a discipline and chooses a belief. That person adopts a philosophical position and is able to defend this position reasonably. The empathetic person evaluates those commitments, taking into account the contributions to other people and society.

A variety of conceptual approaches may be used for understanding or selecting *affective* developmental objectives. Gable (1986, p. 11) has defined four categories of affective characteristics: self-concept, attitudes, interests, and values. Generally, *self-concept* and self-esteem are feelings about oneself; *attitudes* are feelings toward other people, sets of ideas, or social institutions (Thorndike and Hagen, 1969, p. 382); *interests* reflect preferences for selected activities; and *values* relate to beliefs about life goals and ways of life. These four categories are similar in the sense that each is directed toward, or reacts to, some object: the self, the person-made world (for example, a person's ideas about institutions), elements of nature, and other people (for example, life-styles) (Erickson and Wentling, 1976, p. 189).

Chickering's (1969) framework of student development also is largely affective. His seven vectors are (1) developing a sense of competence; (2) managing emotions of sex and aggression; (3) developing autonomy or independence; (4) establishing identity through greater self-confidence and self-awareness; (5) freeing interpersonal relationships by developing tolerance, trust, and intimacy; (6) clarifying vocational and life purposes; (7) developing integrity by behaving in congruence with one's beliefs.

Developmental objectives also have been adopted for divisions of students affairs (Erwin, Menard, and Scott, 1988). These objectives are extensions of Perry's and Chickering's concepts. For an office of financial aid, "to assist students in planning a budget and to help them realize the value of money" (p. 2) relates to value formation and autonomy. The objective cited for career planning and placement—"to help students study, experience, and explore various career options; to help students make career decisions" (p. 4)—shows movement from dualistic thinking to relativistic thinking to commitment. Other developmental objectives are cited for the health center ("to help develop confidence and positive self-perceptions through wellness and health care programs"—p. 5), for admission ("to help students develop tolerance, or to move beyond dualism, by admitting a diversity of students"—p. 4), for residential life ("to help students develop autonomy from family and peers"—p. 7), and for student activities ("to help students develop a sense of identity through involvement with organizations and attendance at workshops, lectures, etc."—p. 11).

In its statement of general education for academic affairs, Virginia Commonwealth University (1988), a public institution, lists five value areas as part of its affective goals: (1) respect for intellectual functioning, as manifested by a commitment to lifelong learning; (2) consideration of others, as manifested by tolerance and altruism; (3) recognition of the role of spirituality in one's life; (4) aspiration toward personal and professional growth; and (5) social and political consciousness and responsibility. Glassboro College (1989) enumerates three developmental objectives as part of its general education program fostered by both academic and student affairs: (1) broadening one's perspective, especially in areas of social and human relations; (2) making informal judgments about issues and relationships; and (3) having personal efficacy or self-confidence.

Specific affective objectives can also be chosen by academic disciplines. For the generic areas of natural sciences, Grandy (1989), Warren (1989), and Nay and Crocker (1970)—using Gable's categories of self-concept, attitudes, interests, and values—list the following objectives: attitudes of honesty, self-direction, and open-mindedness; interest in altruism; values of empathy, or realizing the impact of one's work on other people.

Although most educators would concede the importance of cognitive and affective objectives, these objectives are difficult to assess. First, developmental objectives cannot be measured directly but only indirectly, through behavior that is representative of the attitude or value. Second, it usually takes longer than one semester to inculcate changes in development. Third, the terms or constructs in these areas are still vague and imprecise. Fourth, some people, such as parents, may perceive affective objectives as indoctrination, not education. And fifth, concerns of privacy are appropriately raised. Planning for these issues or concerns beforehand will prevent later difficulties.

Objectives Concerning Skills. Skills are learned outcomes that are both related to and different from knowledge-based and cognitive or affective developmental outcomes. Skills are most commonly enumerated under the purposes of general education, but they also may be listed as academic departmental objectives or student affairs objectives. They are distinct from knowledge in that skills (for example, writing, computer usage, speaking, numeric, and physical skills) are the means by which knowledge is acquired and communicated.

In defining skills related to general education, King's College (Farmer, 1988) has identified eight "transferable skills of liberal learning": critical thinking, creative thinking and problem-solving strategies, effective writing, effective oral communication, quantitative analysis, computer literacy, library and information technology competency, and values awareness. Development of numeric skill is another common institutional objective. At Arizona State University, "global numeric" includes college-level algebra, inferential statistics, and quantitative reasoning (for example, linear programming). In addition to skills across the curriculum, undergraduate programs in the major often adopt particular skill areas as departmental objectives—for example, "Must know the technical writing style used in this discipline" or "Must know how to use existing computer software in this discipline."

At Virginia Military Institute, physical fitness is a large component of the educational program. Therefore, mastery tests were designed to assess students' physical prowess in aerobic and flexibility areas required for entry into the armed services. Applications at other institutions might include less stringent physical fitness requirements, with more emphasis on health and wellness.

Constructing Objectives

How does one construct program objectives? How many should be written, and how long should they be? The process of determining objectives is one of the most beneficial activities in assessment. The average faculty member will assert that he or she is fully aware of program objectives. But having faculty actually write objectives in specific terms is a demanding process, often revealing areas of confusion or imprecision about program intentions. Program objectives should be comprehensive and specific and should state expected changes if possible. The length of a list of departmental objectives varies from discipline to discipline, ranging from a few pages to twenty pages or more. Academic departments do not need to include every concept that is taught in every course. Also, objectives are often broader than what is covered in just a specific course.

When beginning to construct objectives, faculty should first consult their professional organization or other colleagues for examples of objectives. They can also review course syllabi to compile initial lists, but program objectives integrate across several course objectives and are more than a "sum of the parts" of program syllabi. In large departments, it may be impossible to reach unanimity, but a consensus should be achieved. Since the determining of objectives will be controversial within academic departments, often producing healthy discussions about the nature and future of a program, a series of departmental meetings probably will be necessary. Objectives should also be viewed as dynamic. They may be revised when faculty and staff think about how to operationalize them, and revised again when data become available. Banta and Schneider (1988) discuss the secondary effects on program objectives when departments choose to construct their own assessment methods.

Most educators constructing objectives begin with an initial statement that is vague and too global. For instance, a typically phrased objective might read: "Students should be familiar with the principles and theories of the discipline." What does "familiar" mean? It could mean the ability to name some principles, or it could mean some more advanced understanding. Other hard-to-define words commonly used in initial objective drafts include "awareness" and "appreciation." Action-oriented verbs, such as those from the list under Bloom's taxonomy in the earlier part of the chapter, would convey more specific meanings. The substance of the objective should also be specific. The phrase "principles and theories of the discipline" does not state just what principles or what theories the student should learn. This phrase could be interpreted in a variety of ways. Another excessively global statement of objectives is "Learn the history of the discipline." "History" includes a timeless array or broad spectrum of content. What about the history of the discipline should be known? Preferably, the objectives should be stated so that people outside the discipline, such as beginning students, can understand them. In fact, lists of objectives can become advising or recruiting tools for the undecided student because these program objectives are more comprehensive and explanatory than the institution's catalogue.

The establishment of knowledge objectives is relatively easy; the expression of developmental objectives is more difficult. The following higher-order cognitive objectives were written by members of the James Madison University faculty:

Health Sciences: Devise criteria for the selection of personnel qualified to conduct community health in-service programs.

Literature: Appraise the implied and nonliteral meanings of words and phrases within a given context through metaphorical use of language and through irony, understatement, and deliberate incongruity.

Physical Education: Appraise the major concepts of the philosophy of physical education that have led to sprint psychology as an emerging field of study.

Social Work: The student will have the ability to identify, select, adopt, and apply approaches to social work practice from the following list of approaches: structural, task-centered, systems, crisis intervention, psychosocial, social learning, social developmental, Rothman's typology, and conflict based.

Speech Pathology and Audiology: The student will be conceptually and clinically able to differentiate among the following articulation rehabilitation approaches: Van Riper, speech sound discrimination, paired stimulus, modified paired stimulus, and linguistic contrasts.

Objectives sometimes should be expressed in behavioral terms, particularly in programs with physical activities. For example, in dance the following objective could be stated:

> *Dance:* Over the undergraduate period, the student will have performed in a variety of public situations as a dancer, including (1) formal showings or showcases, (2) studio concerts, (3) mainstage or fully produced concerts, and (4) off-campus institutionally related tours.

As mentioned, departments occasionally will specify a skill objective within the context of a major—for example, in a social science or education major program: "The student should use CD-ROM and ERIC searches to obtain documented sources supporting an argument or research strategy." This statement describes a library skill and a computing skill for searching literature electronically. The objective also can be stated in the form of expected changes. In physical education, for instance, it might be expected that graduates will be able to complete a fitness run in a designated time. Suppose this is a stated objective for a major in English: "To learn Shakespeare from films, readings, study-abroad trips, visiting lectures, and theatrical productions." Notice that very little is stated about what is to be learned about Shakespeare. Is it the titles of his works or something deeper? What precisely is to be learned about Shakespeare? In its present form, "to learn Shakespeare" is vague. Also, the words "from films, readings, study-abroad trips, visiting lectures, and theatrical productions" indicate merely *how* Shakespeare should be learned, not *what.*

Some statements of objectives leave out the *what* entirely: "The student should complete Victorian Literature—English 123." What should the students learn or be able to do in this course? It is productive to list the course numbers after each objective, to demonstrate how the objective will be achieved, but listing the courses without the intended outcomes suggests a lack of clear focus and direction in the program.

Environmental Influences

Why do some students reach or achieve the desired outcomes (the outcomes specified in the statements of objectives) while other students do not? Why do some students score higher than other students? Why do some students gain more from college than others? To answer these questions, one must formulate and study various components of the collegiate environment. The campus environment can be described as a set of *functions,* comprising the programs, services, provisions, resources, or methods whereby purposes and objectives are reached (Dressel and Associates, 1961). In the past, people have confused these environmental resources—or *inputs,* as they are called—with objectives and outcomes. For instance, the objective "To ensure small class sizes for ample faculty-student interactions" is really a function or possibly a manipulation of the environment. The student's benefit might be "improved writing ability" or some other objective achieved *as a result of* more instructor feedback.

Inputs, then, are the resources of the institution and the characteristics and abilities that help entering students reach learning and developmental outcomes. Outcomes are what the students actually learn and develop and how well the resources are applied. As was mentioned in Chapter One, assessment is more typically associated with student outcomes, whereas traditional evaluation studies have been associated more with the functions or resources that nurture intended outcomes.

These functions and resources (that is, the courses, activities, services, and influences that make up a campus) are components or subenvironments within the total institutional environment. Each experience or aspect of the campus environment, whether it is a required course or a program in student affairs, can have the potential for increasing or enhancing students' learning or development. For each objective, what are the supporting activities or courses that are expected to help students learn or develop? Ideally, some component of the campus environment, whether it is a course or a student affairs program, should be available for every objective listed. Objectives in this context refer to objectives in the major, in general education, or in student affairs.

Micek and Arney (1974) discuss five categories of the campus environment: instructional, social, organizational, fiscal, and physical. The *instructional* environment includes the teaching or instructional activities—courses, practicums, workshops, field or clinical experiences, and laboratory or studio groups—that affect educational outcomes of students. For the academic program, what are the courses that support the specific program objectives? What are the required courses in a core curriculum that support the liberal studies objectives? Are higher grades in these courses reflective of higher outcomes? If a student completes additional courses beyond the requirements, does this student do better on the outcome measures? This subenvironment is probably the simplest to define because most instructional activities are arranged in an organized fashion around coursework; however, its study has been neglected. Bok (1986a, 1986b), president of Harvard University, believes that higher education should explore why particular students learn more from certain teaching methods than other students do. It is his contention that the identification of differential learning strategies should take precedence over other aspects of the assessment movement. Cross and Angelo (1988) have written a handbook discussing various assessment strategies that are also learning strategies for the classroom teacher.

Within the instructional environment, there may be other logical subdivisions to consider, such as interdisciplinary versus disciplinary courses, honors courses versus regular offerings, lecture versus independent study, computer-assisted instruction versus traditional lectures, or various combinations of courses within an array of required electives. Instructional environments may also occur as noncredit offerings. Does a "planning your career" workshop held in an office of career planning and placement help students become more committed to their major? Does a noncredit workshop about the use of data bases in the library help students better document their research papers?

The remaining categories of subenvironments are more difficult to conceptualize and to define. They require innovative thinking beyond the mere consideration that only in-class offerings affect students' learning and development, but they offer much promise for studying what enhances educational outcomes.

The *social* environment of a campus is its system of interpersonal influences among staff, faculty, administrators, and the students themselves. These influences may be formal, such as the influence of a fraternity or sorority, or informal, such as casual interactions outside class between a faculty member and a student.

If these contacts are systematic and recurring, such as adviser-student relationships, these social subenvironments have the potential for affecting students' developmental and learning levels. For example, does participation in student activities enhance communication and interpersonal skills? Does the grouping of students with similar majors in dorms or designated living areas enhance their learning and development? Magnarella (1975) demonstrated that these living-learning areas do promote greater achievement. The influence of a roommate on students' development also has been demonstrated (Erwin, 1983a). Similarly, minority support groups or offices have been formed in part to offer emotional support for small numbers of minority students making often intimidating adjustments to attending college.

The *fiscal* environment is most commonly studied through the impact of financial aid. In many retention studies, a frequently mentioned reason for leaving an institution is lack of funds for continuing in school. Erwin (1986) and Erwin and Love (1989) explored the association between various financial aid packages and cognitive development. Generally, students who finance a majority of their college expenses gain more from college. In addition, students who receive scholarships or part-time work develop more autonomy or independence than students who receive loans. Other types of fiscal influences might include cooperative programs, work-study arrangements, and internship experiences.

The *organizational* environment reflects the policies and procedures of an institution and may affect students' learning and development. The student-faculty ratio, institutional rules, admissions policies, and retention policies are examples of possible organizational impacts.

The *physical* environment encompasses the architecture and physical design of the campus, which can influence social and personal development and learning (Moos, 1979). It is probably the least studied subenvironment influencing the educational outcomes of students, but at times is worth considering. Areas with possible links to student behavior and performance are various manipulations of classroom space; the restructuring of dormitory rooms—for instance, through movement of modular walls; the availability of lounge and study areas for commuter students; and the convenient placement of microcomputers and libraries near students—for instance, in the dormitories.

Establishing program objectives usually produces changes in a department's curriculum or an office's services before any assessment information is collected. It is also important to remember the distinction between the objectives and the ways that objectives are reached, or what was labeled here as components of the campus environment.

Defining how general education objectives can be accomplished could be the purview of both academic and student affairs staff. Student learning and development in the arts, for example, could be structured conjointly through in-class activities and out-of-class activities. Students could be assigned attendance at designated artistic events or exhibits, which could be discussed in class. Other parallel assignments could be made in other general education areas.

Now that we have determined what is to be assessed, the next two chapters explain how to go about assessing it—namely, by selecting and/or designing appropriate assessment methods.

FOUR

Selecting
Assessment Methods

Once program objectives are established, faculty and student affairs staff should next consider the type of assessment method (such as multiple-choice tests, ratings, or surveys) to be used in obtaining evidence about how well the students are meeting the intended objectives. Before one launches into the lengthy process of designing a new instrument, it is wise to review existing instruments from a testing organization, from professional organizations, or from another institution. As will become apparent in this chapter, each assessment method has it own strengths and weaknesses, and multiple assessment methods are often necessary.

In this book, the terms *assessment method, test,* and *instrument* are used interchangeably, An instrument or a test, in this context, is any systematic method for assessing students' learning or development. More specifically, a test is a "standardized set of questions or other criteria designed to assess knowledge, skills, interests, or other characteristics" of a student (Goldenson, 1984, p. 742). The term *standardized test* implies that the same or equivalent test items or stimuli are given to each student under the same conditions of test administration and scoring. In practice, a test is a series of items written to represent the content domain of interest. These items may also be thought of as observations of a student's behavior.

Norm-Referenced and Criterion-Referenced
Interpretations of Scores or Ratings

The scores or ratings from any assessment method are usually compared in some way for reference purposes. The three varieties of reference are called norm-referenced, criterion-referenced, and self-referenced measures. Faculty and student affairs staff need to know what type of test interpretation would best serve their purpose for assessment. Norm-referenced interpretations report student scores *relative* to those of other students; criterion-referenced interpretations report scores according to an *absolute* standard of achievement (Popham, 1978); and self-referenced measures compare different scores or ratings from the same student. If a department chooses to compare its students' scores with students' scores from other institutions, a norm-referenced approach would be appropriate. If a department wishes to compare its students' scores with a designated level of competency or cutoff standard, a criterion-referenced approach would be more appropriate. Self-referenced measures are used infrequently in higher education assessment programs because they serve only one purpose of assessment—namely, improvement for the individual student.

Most proprietary tests are norm referenced, with percentile ranks reported for reference groups in conjunction with the test scores. Percentile ranks are typically listed in a table ranging from 1 percent to 99 percent, with a test score for each percentile. A percentile rank represents the percentage of persons in a reference group who obtained lower scores (Brown, 1976). For example, if a person is at the 67th percentile, then 67 percent of the persons in that particular norm-referenced group scored at or below that person's score. For a norm-referenced interpretation, there will be at least one reference or norm group; however, it is often useful to report several reference groups, so that a student can be compared with other groups of students who share certain characteristics. Reference groups are often divided by gender, race or ethnic group, educational level, or Carnegie institution type, such as community colleges.

Norm-referenced interpretations serve the useful purpose of allowing an institution to compare the performance of its students with that of students at other institutions. However, a number of problems are apparent with norm-referenced approaches. First, norm-referenced interpretations are often criticized for having little meaning for instructional improvement (Popham, 1978). Some critics claim that nationally standardized tests are constructed too broadly, in an attempt to fit all curricula, so that the scores have little relevance to the specific curriculum of one institution. Second, although norms are supposed to be based on national random samples from the reference group they represent, most norm groups are not random samples but "user-based norms" (Baglin, 1981). User-based norms consist of students from institutions that chose to participate in the testing program. In addition, the students taking the test from a single institution may not be representative of that institution. Volunteer students are usually brighter than typical students. Also, it is not clear what percentile rank demonstrates an acceptable level of performance on any given test at a particular institution. These criticisms relate to the matter of content validity. The comparison of the instrument with the institution's curriculum is an extremely critical step. Faculty need to decide whether the test-curriculum match is adequate and, if it is, what varying levels of performance on the test denote for their institution.

Criterion-referenced interpretations state by their definition that mastery on the test connotes mastery or competence in the instructional knowledge or skill at a given level or standard. Alternative terms such as "domain-based" or "content-based" interpretations have appeared in the literature (for example, Berk, 1978; Baker, Linn, and Quellmalz, 1980). In this book, the terms will be used interchangeably, although distinctions do exist. Criterion-referenced interpretations typically have a designated cutoff level, above which is mastery or passing, below which is failing. Criterion-referenced (or domain- or content-based) interpretations obviously rely heavily on previously defined objectives. A usual college classroom test may be thought of as a criterion-referenced approach. It is tailored to fit the curriculum, with 60 percent correct usually set as a passing grade. Unfortunately, very few tests are designed with criterion-referenced interpretations in mind, and, of course, what is mastery at one institution is not the same at another institution. Often norm-referenced interpretations substitute for criterion-referenced interpretations, with a given percentile becoming the level for mastery.

The concepts of reliability and validity are guidelines for judging the quality of an assessment method under study. Before selecting any test or assessment method, one should review how that method has been used by other groups. Ideally, a test manual has been written that will describe the meaning of the test scores or ratings, explain the process of test design, and provide information about the reliability and validity of the test. Not only people with assigned assessment responsibilities but also faculty or student affairs staff should review this design information and make a determination about the quality and appropriateness of the method for their particular programs. Before using the method to make decisions at their institution, educators sometimes will want to conduct an additional study about some aspect of test validity that has not been previously examined. The mere testing of students or the gathering of assessment data does not guarantee that that information is accurate or worthy for use in decision making for programs or students, even if the test was purchased from a reputable testing firm. Just as assessment information can be used to evaluate programs or individuals, reliability and validity information can be used to evaluate the assessment information for its own inherent quality.

Assessment Formats and Methods

Essentially, there are two broad ways of classifying assessment formats: *selected-response* and *constructed-response* formats (Morris, Fitz-Gibbon, and Lindheim, 1987; Roid and Haladyna, 1982; Robertson, 1989). The selected-response format, also called the recognition format, presents alternative responses, from which the student chooses the correct or preferred answer. Typical selected-response types are multiple-choice, true-false, and matching test items. In the constructed-response format, also called the production format, the student produces an answer or furnishes an "authentic" response to a given stimulus or test question. Typical constructed-response formats are sentence-completion tests, essay questions, and performances or products from "naturalistic" settings. Some writers (for example, Patton, 1987) refer to certain constructed-response stimuli as qualitative; others refer to them as active learning exercises. Generally, an expert is rating a written, visual, verbal, or kinetic form of response from the student (Priestley, 1982). Constructed responses may be actively sought from a task assignment or may be collected unobtrusively from existing portfolios or diaries (Webb, Campbell, Schwartz, and Sechrest, 1966). Selected-response formats are associated with either locally designed or commercially procured tests, while constructed-response formats usually are locally designed.

Some writers believe that constructed responses represent more realistic behavior (Fitzpatrick and Morrison, 1971); however, other authors, such as Ebel (1979), view selected-response formats as equally viable measures of the learning process. Individual educators and departments must decide for themselves their format of choice, but many departments use a combination of formats because of their multiple objectives.

Multiple-choice tests are well known to faculty because of their ease in scoring, their high reliability, and their ability to cover many topics efficiently. They are perhaps most suitable for measuring "reiteration," or basic facts and principles of a discipline. Multiple-choice tests can also be suitable, with careful reflection, for assessing higher-order thinking skills (Miller, Williams, and Haladyna, 1978).

On most campuses, the reliability of multiple-choice tests can be determined through a locally written test-scoring software program or a popular statistical computing package. Furthermore, most of these software programs furnish information about each test item, and this information can be used to improve the test's reliability. Tips on writing and improving multiple-choice items will be provided in the next chapter.

Assessment activities have also reinforced the need to supplement the traditional selected-response tests with constructed-response measures. That is, a student's behavior is observed and assessed in a naturalistic setting or under realistic conditions—for instance, in interviews or on open-ended questionnaires. Observations also can be made of students' *performances* (for example, in a dance recital, a concert, a golf game, or a therapy session), *processes* (for example, a research study, a chemical analysis, or any other assignment that elicits critical-thinking and problem-solving faculties), _products_ (paintings or sculptures, stories or articles, a radio or television broadcast, blueprints, maps, computer programs, or chemical compounds), _records_ (for instance, recommendations, résumés, practicum evaluations, or case notes), and _social-personal traits_ (such as honesty, persistence, independence, planning ability, or decision-making style).

Prior expectations of the students' behaviors or characteristics are then systematically assessed through a checklist or rating scale. These assessed observations are less intrusive and more tied to skills and development than selected-response measures are. Consequently, assessments based on observations of a student's behavior or characteristics are more authentic than assessments based on selected-response formats.

For some educators (Alverno College Faculty, 1979; Fitzpatrick and Morrison, 1971), the assessment situation should be as "real life" oriented as possible. For example, a dance major would be expected to perform modern and ballet dances. Historical preservation majors at Mary Washington College (Hudgins, 1988) might be expected to complete a federal application for preservation of a historical building. The reality of the exercise or situation provides motivation for the student to do well, relevance of assessment to instruction, and excellent feedback about areas for program improvement. Ratings are used to evaluate writing ability as well as course content.

Ratings naturally lend themselves to artistic performances, where the expected outcome can be evaluated within the context of instruction and service. That is, if the goal of a program culminates in a student's producing an artistic masterpiece that encompasses all past knowledge and training, then assessment should occur within that context of the student's education. In other words, a multiple-choice test should not be used as the only method of evaluating artistic ability if an artistic product is also available.

Ratings are also appropriate for projects typically assigned as capstone experiences in the senior year. Such senior projects might include case studies typically found in schools of business, construction projects in architecture or engineering, a science interview conducted in the laboratory, or portfolios collected by the student.

Clinical observations of teaching abilities or therapeutic skills are convenient settings for performance ratings. Much attention is now being devoted to evaluating a teaching style in the classroom, not just the student's knowledge of what to teach (Shulman, 1987). Other disciplines, such as social work and nursing, use ratings to evaluate students' skills in counseling and therapy or in the health profession. Other naturalistic skills, such as physical fitness or speaking skills, also can be readily evaluated through ratings. Majors in physical education are often expected to have competencies in sports and in other areas requiring fitness and flexibility. Moreover, public-speaking skills must always be rated in context.

The oral test or interview is a well-established method for evaluating undergraduate student performance. Exit interviews of students enable faculty committees or department heads to probe for a student's depth of understanding. Although a time-consuming vehicle, the in-depth interview is occasionally found in divisions of student affairs where personal and social development constructs are evaluated. See Mines (1982) for further examples of the use of the structured interview in student development.

Anecdotal records often can serve as useful assessment products for review. For example, in social work practicums and in student-teaching settings, supervisors write narrative reports about the activities and performances of student trainees in their work settings. These narrative records can provide the basis for content analysis about specific aspects of the student's performance.

Finally, quantitative problems are natural assessment products for students in fields such as mathematics, physics, and engineering. Sometimes multiple-choice tests are used, but many faculty prefer problems or proofs where solutions can be rated for degrees of partial credit.

Ratings are a quantitative source of assessment information. Quantifiability is a basic requirement for assessment information in many states—for example, in Virginia. As will be discussed in Chapter Seven, the analysis of ratings poses some unique problems. However, the advantage of ratings is that they are suitable for calculating reliability. This possibility—plus the intrinsic value of rating students in the context of their education through the various assessment products—makes ratings a particularly valuable assessment method.

The use of ratings and checklists is emerging as a popular alternative to traditional multiple-choice tests for faculty and student affairs staff, because ratings are familiar to educators and are natural consequences of many assessment-related performances and products. Moreover, ratings have the advantage of being in quantitative form, which satisfies many state and accrediting association mandates about the form of assessment data. In the next chapter, types of rating scales and checklists are defined and explained further.

Reliability

"Reliability" refers to the consistency, precision, and dependability of our measurements. How clearly focused is the assessment information? Validity, the partner of reliability, deals with the worth, or applicability, of these measurements for one's stated objectives. How well does a test measure what it is supposed to measure? Does it provide information appropriate to its purpose? For instance, consider the process of a bird watcher who seeks to identify a falcon in flight. The precision of the binoculars or the ability to focus clearly on the distant object may be linked to reliability. The bird watcher's ability to discern whether the object already in focus is a bird, or indeed a falcon, constitutes validity. The clarity with which we measure must first be established before the worth of any measurement can be determined. In other words, we must determine that reliability is adequate before we can examine validity. Reliability is a necessary condition for validity. However, for assessment information to be useful in decision making, an assessment method must have both good reliability and evidence of validity.

As an indicator of the importance of reliability, imagine the practice of asking several questions of a student to obtain his or her true ability in some aspect of development. The person making the assessment would not want to rely on one or two test questions or observations of student behavior to judge the level of development or ability. Instead, that person would collect a number of observations or pose a number of test questions for greater fairness. This process of collecting several observations about a similar set of educational objectives is simply the strengthening of reliability, or the accuracy of measurement.

Sources of Error. How do we know whether an assessment method is reliable? The most common sources of errors of measurement (lack of reliability) usually come from the student or a test taker, from the assessment instrument, and from the conditions of assessment administration. Once identified, these errors of measurement should be reduced to improve the quality of the assessment information.

Errors arising from the student typically result from the lack of motivation to take assessment seriously; from prior experience with being evaluated; or from test anxiety, coaching, and certain physiological variables (Brown, 1976). For example, if a student is tired or sick, he or she will probably not furnish a typical test performance on that particular day. Unfortunately, many of these student factors are not controllable by the institution. Some steps that can be taken will be discussed later.

A second source of error in assessment comes from the particular assessment instrument. For instance, in a multiple-choice test, the test items may be ambiguously worded. If the test questions are not clearly written and could be interpreted in a variety of ways, the test information will not be consistent or reliable. If a rating scale is confusing or vague, the raters will not react to the same observations in a similar manner. For example, consider the question "Is the proposal well ordered, specific, and relevant?" The question asks the rater to consider three components of a proposal, not just one. What is the rater to do if the proposal is strong in two of the components but weak in a third? Furthermore, words such as *relevant* can mean different things to different people.

Another problem has to do with the representativeness of test items. For example, if two test forms differ in their emphasis on program content, inconsistent scores may result. More specifically, if a testing firm sends a faculty two forms of the same test for its students, and one form contains more recent material about the discipline than the other, then scores are likely to differ on the two test forms. Most problems of measurement arising from the assessment instrument can be prevented through proper instrument selection or through careful wording of the instrument.

A third common source of error arises from the conditions of assessment administration. The ways in which tests are administered are typically dismissed as insignificant, but research (Anastasi, 1988) has suggested that varying the style of test administration procedures also produces varying scores. Educators, of course, want their results to differ because of various types of educational programs, not because of the conditions of test administration. If the conditions of test administration are not uniform for all students, students' responses to the test may vary according to the way the test was administered, and not according to the students' true ability. Consider a general education assessment program that schedules several makeup sessions to accommodate students' schedules. If one group is given an extra fifteen minutes to complete a task, while other students are not, differences in scores or ratings may be attributable to more time, not to higher ability.

The greater the error in any assessment information, the less reliable it is, and the less likely it is to be useful. Admittedly, any assessment method, and therefore any measurement of human behavior or performance, contains error or is unreliable to some degree. Some educators claim that certain educational objectives, such as those in the affective domain, cannot be clearly or reliably measured; and some affective measures do contain more measurement error than certain subject matter objectives contain. The differences in reliability among several tests are caused in part by the varying degree of specificity for the content areas or objectives to be measured. Usually, subject matter objectives are easier to define than affective objectives. In practice, objectives that are stated vaguely or too globally usually result in unreliable methods. For the most part, the degree of reliability reflects the clarity of the educational objectives that have been stated.

Types of Reliability. Four types of reliability are most commonly considered by reviewers of standardized instruments. The first type of reliability is *stability,* usually described in a test manual as test-retest reliability. If the same test is readministered to the same students within a short period of time, such as two weeks, their scores should be highly similar, or stable. Both norm-referenced and criterion-referenced tests should have high levels of test-retest reliability.

A second type of reliability is _equivalence_, or the degree of similarity of results among alternate forms of the same test. Standardized tests often are offered in various forms, to guard against the possibility that a person might remember test questions from one administration to the next. To what degree do the differing forms of the test produce the same or similar scores? Again, tests interpreted as both criterion-referenced and norm-referenced should have high levels of equivalence if different forms are offered.

Another type of reliability is *homogeneity or internal consistency,* the interrelatedness of the test items used to measure a given dimension of learning and development. Do the items on the given assessment instrument measure the same characteristic? Internal consistency coefficients can be found for both cognitive and affective instruments. Of course, a given assessment instrument may have several subscales or subtests; the test items in each subscale or subtest should measure similar facets of the intended characteristic or content domain. For example, the Educational Testing Service's (1988) Major Field Achievement Test in history has two subscores, European History and United States History, instead of a single score. The European History subtest covers the history of this region from the medieval period to the twentieth century, and no questions about non-European history should be a part of this subtest. If heterogeneous items cannot be avoided, then measures of stability or equivalence should be used, instead of internal consistency, to guage reliability. Internal consistency estimates are usually associated most closely with norm-referenced approaches.

A final type of reliability, called _interrater reliability,_ pertains to the consistency with which raters evaluate a single performance of a given group of students. In higher education, ratings are commonly used because faculty are familiar with using ratings in the grading process and because certain assessment areas, such as artistic performance or writing, cannot be evaluated quantitatively unless rating scales are used. Unfortunately, two or more raters do not always perceive students in the same way, understand the rating items exactly the same way, or rate student performance according to the same measure. No one can expect faculty ratings to be identical, but high agreement is important if the information is to be useful. These problems produce varying rating results, or inconsistencies in measurement, that are irrelevant to the intended ability or characteristic of the student.

One explanation for the existence of today's assessment activities is the perceived unreliability or inconsistency of the single rater, the instructor, in giving grades. For ratings to be accurate, the possible variation in raters must be examined.

Subject matter achievement tests from the major testing organizations usually provide information about both stability (test-retest) and equivalence (form-to-form) reliabilities. Stability and equivalence reliabilities are typically estimated through statistical techniques called coefficients of reliability, which range in value from 0 to 1.0. A value of 1.0 suggests perfect reliability, something never obtained in practice; a value of 0 means that there is no reliability—that is, no relationship between a student's score on the first and second administrations of the tests, or between scores on the administration of two forms of the test. If assessment results are to be used for group or program purposes, reliability coefficients of .60 or above are generally acceptable. If one wishes to report results back to individual students, greater precision (.70 or more) is necessary. Table 2 illustrates reliability estimates for the Educational Testing Service's Major Field Achievement Tests. Another testing program for consideration is the Project for Area Concentration Achievement Testing, by Tony Golden at Austin Peay University. Although much test design work is yet to be done, the project covers the disciplines of political science, psychology, social work, agriculture, art, biology, and literature in English.

The calculation of reliability with the homogeneity approach is usually based on two different formulas, depending on the type of scoring method. If an answer is scored as either correct or incorrect, internal consistency reliability should be determined with the Kuder-Richardson-20 formula. This method is used with essentially most proprietary achievement tests. If the instrument has more than one correct answer per test item, such as partial credit or

**Table 2. Reliability Estimates for Major Field Achievement Tests,
Educational Testing Service.**

Major Field Achievement Test	Reliability Coefficient
Biology (total score)	.92
cellular and subcellular biology	.81
organismal biology	.80
population biology; ecology and evolution	.84
Business	.91
Chemistry	.91
Computer Science	.85
Economics (total score)	.90
microeconomics	.75
macroeconomics	.76
Education	.92
Engineering (total score)	.92
engineering	.86
mathematics	.86
Geology (total score)	.93
stratigraphy, sedimentology, paleontology, and geomorphology	.79
structural geology and geophysics	.84
mineralogy, petrology, and geochemistry	.83
History (total score)	.90
European history	.85
United States history	.81
Literature in English	.94
Mathematics	.84
Music Theory and History (total score)	.91
theory	.82
history and literature	.86
Physics	.90
Political Science	.85
Psychology (total score)	.91
experimental psychology	.80
social psychology	.84
Sociology	.88

Source: Data obtained from Educational Testing Service, 1990.

weighted alternatives for scoring, then Cronbach's (1951) coefficient of internal consistency would provide the necessary reliability information. Although more complex methods exist in measurement theory (Crocker and Algina, 1986), reliability estimates derived from these methods usually will appear in the test manuals of the various commercially available tests. If reliability information is missing from a test manual, it should be requested from the test's author, or the test should be administered only as an experiment.

The interpretation of interrater reliability (discussed in Chapter Five) is the same as for the prior three types of reliabilities. Interrater reliabilities below, say, .70 are suspect as to their accuracy.

In the area of item discrimination, each item is studied for its power to discriminate between high and low scorers. Item discrimination indexes are calculated to determine the correlation between the probability of answering an item correctly and the total score on the remaining part of the test. These point-biserial correlation coefficients range from -1.0, a negative relationship, to +1.0, a perfect positive relationship. If the test items measuring a single construct are highly interrelated or homogeneous, the hypothesis that the test is measuring a single dimension of a construct is supported. The assumption here is that homogeneity or internal consistency implies a clear, singular definition of the construct under study. Partially because of this view of reliability, many test designers calculate reliability coefficients using a formula for internal consistency. More sophisticated statistical analyses, such as factor analysis, are also used with large samples to confirm relationships among test items.

Validity

As mentioned, validity addresses the question "Does the test or other assessment instrument measure what it is supposed to measure?" Because one cannot see a person's abilities or inner traits of development directly, it is difficult or impossible to verify with complete certainty that any method measures these hidden attributes. Because of this uncertainty, some critics believe that no attempts at assessment should take place. But even though no assessment effort is perfectly reliable or valid, valuable information can still be collected and used for improving educational courses and programs.

Whereas reliability can be determined through a quantitative index that ranges from 0 or no reliability to 1.0 or perfect reliability, validity is not so easy to determine with any comparable numerical scale. Validity must be judged according to the application of each use of the method. Has the method successfully measured what it was intended to measure? No test or any other assessment method can be validated for all applications, settings, or uses. In fact, validity rests in the hands of the individual user, not just with the test designer. For instance, a test may have supporting validity evidence at one institution but not at another institution. The validity of an assessment method is never proved absolutely; it can only be supported by an accumulation of evidence from several categories. The more evidence is available, the more credible is the assessment method. This inferential process for determining validity is similar to measurement in other sciences. For example, "Geologists mapping subterranean rock formations, particle physicists estimating the energy of subatomic particles, and biologists describing generic structures must also rely on indirect measurement methods" (Hogan and Nicholson, 1988, p. 622).

Traditionally, validity has been categorized as a triad of content, criterion-related, and construct validity types (Brown, 1976). However, a recent study suggests a more complex array of possible validity evidence studies. For any assessment method to be used in decision making, the following categories (Messick, 1989, p. 6) should be considered:

1. Content relevance and representativeness.
2. Internal test structure.
3. External test structure.
4. Process of probing responses.
5. Test's similarities and differences over time and across groups and settings.
6. Value implications and social consequences.

These six categories, which rely both on expert judgment and on empirical studies, will be discussed throughout this section.

Content relevance and representativeness are typically dem- /
onstrated through the systematic matching of each test item with
stated program objectives. Some writers, such as Anastasi (1988), use
the term *domain* instead of *educational objectives* to describe what
the test is supposed to measure. Whichever term is used, the selected
test should be a representative sample from those objectives or that
domain. The test should cover what the program covered and
should place emphasis in proportion to the program's emphases.
For example, in a history major that emphasized Asian history, one
would not want to choose a test that contained few or no questions
about Asian history. Proprietary exams often do not reflect certain
emphases of programs at particular institutions. Some tests are not
sufficiently up to date to include new knowledge being taught in
a program. An institution should attend to the full range of content
of an instrument designed outside the institution, in order to guard
against inappropriate test selection.

Institutions rushing into assessment activities often skip this
step of determining content relevance and representativeness. They
will lease a test off the market without giving any consideration to
how well that test fits the institution's program. If the students score
lower than expected on the test, a common reaction is to revise the
curriculum, or subtly "start teaching to the test."

Tests may be reliable but not valid for a particular program.
For instance, the American College Testing Program's (ACT) test
battery on general education, called the College Outcome Measures
Project (COMP), has high internal consistency reliability estimates
for its "selective response forms" (Forrest and Steele, 1982). However, its validity or appropriateness for a particular institution's
curriculum depends on the definition or objectives of general education at that institution. How well does the ACT-COMP, in this
example, match with the institution's general education objectives?
If the fit between objectives and test is high, then the test is content-
valid for that program. If the fit between program objectives and test
is poor, then the test is not relevant for the particular program.

Some critics of off the shelf tests will make sweeping state-
ments about the inappropriateness of certain tests for all programs.
Such opinions ignore the great differences in academic programs.
Even though a reliable test did not reveal changes in student abilities

at a particular institution, it still could be a useful measurement device at another institution. Perhaps the test was chosen without regard to the goals of the first institution's program.

Two examples, one global and one more specific, will be given here to illustrate the process of content review, or matching the purposes of a test with the objectives of a program. In the global example, consider again the selection of a test to measure general education. General education, as its name suggests, can encompass a wide array of educational objectives that may differ greatly from institution to institution. Tests of general education likewise reflect differing conceptualizations of general education. Three of these tests of general education are the ACT-COMP, the Educational Testing Service's Academic Profile (ETS-AP), and Riverside Publishing's College BASE.

The ACT-COMP takes a life skills or "civic competence" approach (Forrest, 1979) to general education. With its subscales of "Functioning Within Social Institutions," "Using the Arts," and "Solving Problems," it attempts to tap abilities that are important in everyday life for roles of "consumer, voter, parent, volunteer, and spouse." The ETS-AP takes a more content- or curriculum-oriented approach to general education. It does have skill subscales, as the ACT-COMP does; but it also has subscales of "Humanities," "Social Science," and "Natural Science," which describe general categories in a liberal studies curriculum. College BASE (Osterlind, 1989) has four content areas (English, mathematics, science, and social studies) and three cognitive competencies (called interpretive reasoning, strategic reasoning, and adaptive reasoning). Subscores (called cluster scores) are reported within each content area, and criterion levels are reported as high, middle, or low for twenty-three skills.

Depending on its definition of general education, an institution could select any one of these instruments, or something else, to measure its particular view or conceptualization of general education. From a global perspective, some instruments can be eliminated on the basis of their general description. Remaining instruments for consideration should also be scrutinized closely, which leads to the second example. This example describes what should be a common procedure for academic departments that are studying available instruments on the market from testing organizations. Essentially, that procedure is to match systematically each item from the test with the program's objectives. Table 3 gives an example from the discipline of biology.

The department has prepared a synopsis of its subject matter objectives, as shown in Table 3. The numbers to the left of the objectives indicate how many test items from a fictitious exam in biology relate to each program objective. Obviously, the higher numbers mean good coverage of a particular subject matter objec-

Table 3. Determining Content Validity: Synopsis of Undergraduate Biology Objectives for Fictitious Biology Test.

Number of Test Items	Subject Matter Objectives
	a. Molecular and Cellular Biology
3	1) The origin of life.
8	2) Chemical composition of organism; macromolecular structure.
11	3) Cell structure and function; metabolism; prokaryotic v. eukaryotic cells.
8	4) Cell cycles, evolution and morphogenesis.
7	5) Enzymes.
9	6) Energy transformations.
16	7) Flow of genetic information.
	b. Organismal Biology
19	1) A comparative understanding of structure and function in vascular and nonvascular plants.
4	2) Plant reproduction and development.
30	3) Structure and function in vertebrate and invertebrate animals, including a comparative understanding of their systems.
11	4) Animal reproduction and development.
8	5) Principles of heredity.
0	6) Systematics and taxonomic principles.
12	7) Behavior of animals.
8	8) An introduction to microbial biology.
	c. Population Biology
1	1) Ecosystem concept.
5	2) Biogeochemical cycling.
15	3) Population and community ecology.
14	4) Habitat and the niche.
5	5) Process of natural selection.
15	6) Principles of evolution; speciation.

tive. A low number possibly means inadequate emphasis on that area on the test. For example, the objective "ecosystem" has only one test item, and the objective "systematics and taxonomic principles" has no items. If too many objectives have too few items for representation, the test will have low content validity for that particular program. Of course, that judgment is to be made by faculty from that program who have reviewed each item of the test. If only a few categories have low numbers of test items, the standardized test might still be chosen; however, a locally designed method may be needed to supplement this test for those objectives with inadequate coverage.

Another important use of the concept of validity is in the measurement of developmental constructs, or the degree to which a scale or a test measures a personal characteristic, trait, quality, or concept. Like learning, developmental constructs are not directly observable in behavior except through an accumulation of observations of a variety of behaviors. Often, the behaviors are indirect indicators of that intended construct. For example, leadership is a construct commonly listed in many educational goal statements; yet no single indicator of behavior can be linked to leadership. Leadership could be defined as speaking ability, independence of thinking, ability to set goals, and so on (Committee to Develop Standards for Educational and Psychological Testing, 1985). Other developmental constructs are moral development, critical thinking, career decisiveness, identity, values, and maturity. Measurement of these areas, as was discussed earlier, is perhaps more difficult than that of subject matter objectives, but it is nonetheless important and necessary for some programs. These developmental objectives must be described very precisely, since they can be understood in a variety of ways or have multiple interpretations. Every effort must be made to eliminate as much confusion as possible.

Validity evidence of *internal test structure* is typically demonstrated through intercorrelations among items covering the same content domain. For item discrimination approaches, students who score well on the test under study should be able to answer individual test items correctly. Comparatively, students from that same sample who score low on the test overall would be expected to miss most items. This concept is similar to that of internal consistency in reliability.

One can also study internal test structure by examining the difficulty levels of each test item or rating item. Difficulty is usually operationalized as the proportion or percentage of students who passed or performed successfully on a given item. For norm-referenced interpretations, the most reliable results are produced when about half of the students answer the items correctly. For criterion-referenced interpretations, a high proportion of students, say 80–90 percent, should answer each item successfully if they have mastered the relevant program or course.

Validity evidence for the *external test structure* is necessary when the educator wishes to compare test scores or ratings with other measures or related variables. For example, one would expect a locally constructed test of physics to produce scores somewhat similar to those obtained on a standardized test such as the Educational Testing Service's (1988) Major Field Achievement Test in physics. Other measures, such as external measures of success or achievement, are often available as criteria. Typical educational criteria might include grades, retention status, acceptance into or performance in graduate school, performance on a postgraduate professional examination, the opinions of outside judges or expert ratings, ratings of job performance, and other behavioral indications of successful citizenship or functioning in society.

Determining acceptable criteria for tests may be as difficult as determining useful assessment indicators of undergraduate learning and development. In some disciplines, institutions might be able to compare assessment data collected during students' undergraduate years with behaviors exhibited later as alumni. Greater learning and development at the institution should be predictive of future success in the workplace or in society. For example, as Williams, Tiller, Herring, and Scheiner (1988) say from the point of view of accounting faculty, "Oral communication skills of staff accountants, as gauged by our measure, are positively associated with client satisfaction and cooperativeness, and negatively associated with client attrition" (p. 167). It should be remembered that the issues of reliability and validity still apply to criteria and must be taken into consideration because criteria, too, are measures of human performance.

Scores and ratings may also differ according to certain background variables. For example, scores or ratings in a subject matter or skill test in the major should be higher for graduate students than for undergraduate students. If criteria or other assessment measures are available, similar measures should converge or exhibit similar patterns. For example, physicians' ratings of student nurses should be similar to the nursing faculty's ratings of the same nurses on the same skills.

Perhaps the most common example of a criterion-related study is the study that investigates the usefulness of an admissions or basic skills test in predicting college grades or retention. This type of study is coming under criticism from some educators because grades are no longer considered reliable and valid criteria (Goldman and Slaughter, 1976). Nevertheless, the relationship of an admissions test, such as the Scholastic Aptitude Test (SAT), to the criterion of freshman grade point average can be studied. SAT subscores used as predictors in the study could be the reading, vocabulary, and mathematics subscores and the Test of Standard Written English subscore. If students who scored higher on the SAT subscores also had higher grades, the SAT would have some usefulness in predicting how well students will succeed in college. If a strong relationship existed between SAT scores and grades, the SAT would have criterion-related validity for that particular institution and could be used perhaps for freshman advising.

Traditionally, investigations of external structural validity have attempted to determine whether the worth or value of a program or educational service could be proved with a different group of students in another setting. For example, the value of a drug awareness program could be tested by its implementation and study at another institution. Does it work elsewhere? For some institutions, the transferability of a program is not a concern; however, the assessment method is deemed more powerful if it includes an external element to it. For instance, if loyal faculty are rating local students' performance or product, the use of an external judge or examiner could strengthen the ratings. This external judge could be a visiting professor or an outside consultant in the discipline (Fong, 1987).

Validity evidence for *probing the process* is typically sought 4 at two points during any test or scale construction period. First, after a pool of test items is written, a few students may be asked to report orally how they interpret the words and meaning behind each test question. Are the students' interpretations consistent with the intent of the test designer? For rating scales, raters should have trial runs in which each rater describes how a sample case would be rated. Is each rater keying on the same appropriate behaviors? Is each rater interpreting the rating scale items in a similar fashion? Often, test items or rating scale items need to be added or modified as a part of this process. At the second point of probing the process, data have already been collected on the designated group of students, such as graduating seniors, and a subset of these students can be targeted for further probing. For example, students who scored very high or very low, or students who did not change or who changed greatly over time, might be interviewed to uncover reasons for their unique abilities or development. A pattern might be discovered that can be examined more systematically in some future assessment study.

Validity evidence related to *expected performance similarities and differences* should be studied longitudinally and in various 5 groups and settings. That is, some outcome measures should increase over time, as Astin (1974, 1982) stated in his value-added or talent development approach. Also, certain subgroups of students should have higher outcome scores on the average than other subgroups of students. Developmental scores and ratings usually show predictable changes over the undergraduate years. For example, identity (Erwin and Delworth, 1980) typically drops during the freshman year because of the culture shock of college, whereas an undergraduate's autonomy or independence should increase between entering freshman and senior years. In fact, most developmental dimensions should increase over the undergraduate years. (The technical problems in analyzing such changes will be discussed in Chapter Seven.) Faculty may also wish to examine trends over time; however, since most students enter college with very little knowledge of their major discipline, the value-added approach is unnecessary.

An outcome instrument should be able to differentiate among predicted subgroups of students. For example, if a test of moral development is administered to students who have completed an ethics course and to another group of students who have been caught stealing books from the library, the moral development tests should exhibit markedly different averages between the two groups of students. Students taught ethics should presumably score higher on the average in moral development than students who steal. Again, in the area of leadership, one would expect students who have held leadership positions in campus organizations to have higher scores on a leadership test than students who have not held leadership positions. As a last example, if an institution lists the developmental objective of autonomy, seniors who have financed their college education should score higher in autonomy than students who depended on their parents for total financial support.

A locally designed departmental test in a discipline should produce similar scores when the test is transported to students in the same major at a similar institution. Faculty would also expect students with higher grades to do better on the assessment method of interest than students with lower grades. Other differences should also be exhibited among students with varying exposures to instruction or program intervention. Students who have completed certain courses might be expected to score or rate higher than other students. Students who have been to the counseling center or to the career development service might be more committed or certain in their career choice. As the reader probably has already noted, this approach to validity is similar to examining external test structure.

A final aspect of validity concerns the _social consequences_ of decisions based on assessment data. Although other approaches to validity may have demonstrated support for use of a given method, the question of social consequences should always be investigated. If a test or rating scale discriminates against certain groups of people, such as minorities or women, that test or scale should be considered suspect. For example, if a disproportionate number of black students are prohibited from advancing to the junior year because of their scores on a basic skills test, that test should not be used further unless investigators can determine that it does not discriminate unfairly against these black students. Issues of test bias are complex (Cole and Moss, 1989); however, the point to be made here is that the possible adverse impact of the use of some scores or ratings, particularly in institution-wide or statewide assessment programs, always should be considered.

No single piece of validity evidence is sufficient to support the use of assessment information for decision making. The use of multiple data collection strategies can overcome the deficiencies of any single approach, as was noted by Campbell and Fiske (1959) in their multitrait-multimethod matrix discussions. Denzin (1978) expands this idea further with his concept of triangulation of data, methods, theories, and investigators. Triangulation is simply the building of multiple sources of information or ideas to support a central finding or theme. Data triangulation means the use of multiple samples of students. Such student samples might come from different years of graduation, different semesters of graduation, or different institutions. Other samples, for use as a comparison group, might come from a nearby community of persons not attending college. Methodological triangulation entails multiple methods, such as multiple-choice tests, rating scales, and surveys. Theory triangulation would include diverse conceptual perspectives to interpret a set of data. In explaining students' development over the undergraduate years, Chickering (1969), Heath (1968, 1977), and Perry (1970) use these conceptual perspectives. Finally, investigator triangulation means that different interpreters of the data are used. These interpreters might be different groups of faculty within a single department, faculty in the same discipline at a different institution, faculty or staff outside one's department, assessment personnel, or administrators.

Guidelines for Selecting Instruments

In the process of selecting an instrument to assess a program's stated objectives, attention should be balanced equally between studies of reliability and validity. Traditionally, analysis of reliability comes first, because a test's worth is limited by its preciseness. That is, a test's validity is limited by its degree of reliability. Therefore, if a test has low reliability, that test cannot consistently measure a specified body of content, predict a criterion, or exhibit differences among groups of students with different training or education.

As a brief summary of this chapter, the following guidelines are provided for faculty or staff to consider in instrument selection:

1. Is there evidence for reliability? Is the type of reliability appropriate for the type of assessment method?
2. Are the items of the test or rating scale keyed to specific program objectives? Are the items keyed to developmental levels, such as reiteration or application?
3. Have gender, cultural, ethnic, and geographical biases been minimized?
4. Are the directions for administration clear? Are the rules for scoring the responses and behaviors clear?
5. Is the sample for standardization and initial design of the instrument clearly described?
6. Are percentiles provided, with sample descriptions, for norm-referenced interpretations?
7. Are mastery cutoff scores or rating levels provided for criterion-referenced interpretations?
8. What evidence for validity exists? Is the level of difficulty appropriate for the intended program?
9. Are the scores or ratings reported in a form that is useful for the program? For example, some tests report only a total score, which may not be useful for diagnostic purposes. What is needed are subscores for assessing various components of the program.

FIVE

Designing New Methods
to Fit Institutional Needs

This chapter reviews several sources of assessment information and offers techniques for designing reliable and valid assessment instruments. Designing one's own instruments is hard work—much harder than, for example, constructing a classroom test. Therefore, the typical faculty member or student affairs staff should allow ample time for the process. Such work and commitment can be rewarded with assessment feedback tailored to specific program needs. Most of us need not limit ourselves to selecting multiple-choice tests as our only assessment method. In fact, no assessment program should be limited to the use of just one assessment method. Programs have multiple objectives, so why not multiple methods? Furthermore, each assessment method has its own set of problems, or errors of measurement. For example, information obtained from an oral test may be tainted by the student's anxiety about speaking under pressure; this might not be a problem with another method. A combination of diverse assessment methods offsets the problems of any one method and presents a consensus about program effectiveness from numerous methodological perspectives.

Designing Selected-Response Measures

Before test questions or rating items are written, a *table of specifications* or blueprint of the test should be outlined. How many subtopics, subareas, or subtests are needed for feedback within the program? For most programs, a single score for each student is insufficient, because such a score does not furnish diagnostic feedback about the various components of the program. On the other hand, a department probably should not design a subscore for every required course. Most departments may find that four to six subscales or subscores are ample for a program. Most subscales will encompass material from at least two courses, and different assessment methods will supply different subscales. For example, a multiple-choice examination may supply three or four subscores; a writing sample, a writing subscore; and a senior project, another two or three subscores for each student.

Types of Organizational Designs. A table of specifications organizes the educational information by content, program emphasis, and developmental level. Table 4 provides examples of tables of specifications for library competency within an English major (Cameron, Chappell, and Riordan, 1989) and for physics (Taylor and Erwin, 1989). Different subscores would be reported for each student in these various subtopics. Obviously, one can deduce the program emphasis by observing the number of test questions provided for each subtopic.

It should be cautioned here that the number of test questions, multiple-choice items, or rating items influences the reliability of each subtopic. As mentioned in Chapter Three, a subscore comprised of only two or three test questions is a risky estimate, usually reflected by a low reliability coefficient. Generally, the greater the number of test questions, the greater the reliability. Allen and Yen (1979) describe in greater detail the relationship between reliability and test length.

Another way to organize test questions and methods is by cognitive developmental levels, as shown in Table 5. The numbers reflect the desired degree of emphasis in the test by both dimensions of content and cognitive level. In some cells, one will notice that there are no items. For example, there was no intention to test any "applications" in the "history of physical education and sports." Similarly, in the content category of "creating behavior changes," all three test items were directed at the two highest cognitive levels:

Table 4. Tables of Specifications.

Areas Assessed	Number of Items
1. Library Competencies for English Literature Majors	
Library on-line catalogue (commands and search strategies)	5
Reference room resources (computerized indexes, dictionaries, and encyclopedias)	6
Locations of library resources (stacks, periodicals, and special collections)	4
English and literature resources	
MLA International Bibliography	5
Literature bibliographies and aids (specialized guides, indexes, and bibliographies)	7
Library services (interlibrary loan and reserves)	2
2. Physics Test	
Mechanics	16
Electricity and magnetism	32
Heat and thermodynamics	28
Optics	12
Electronics	16
Modern physics	28
Math methods	5
Physics electives	47

Source: Data obtained from Cameron, Chappell, and Riordan, 1989 and Taylor and Erwin, 1989.

Bloom's "synthesis and evaluation." This particular test was multiple choice; however, this table of specifications could also apply to other types of assessment methods, such as ratings. In fact, this department supplemented some "missing" cells in "synthesis and evaluation" with behavioral rating scales of fitness and of a wellness program.

A final example, drawn from my own institution, is shown in Figure 1: the design of a test in the liberal studies or general education area of philosophy and religion. This example illustrates the assessment of developmental processes, not subject matter content, using a selection-response format. Three processes (egocentrism, ethnocentrism, and global reasoning) and three views of the

Table 5. Tables of Specifications: Cognitive Categories for Physical Education Majors.

Content Area	Knowledge[a]	Comprehension	Application	Analysis	Synthesis and Evaluation
Kinesiology	1[b]	1	6	4	2
Exercise physiology and conditioning	7	5		5	4
Motor learning and development		6	4	4	
Psychology and sociology		8	1	3	2
History of P.E. and sports	1	2			1
Philosophy of P.E. and sports		1		2	1
Human anatomy and physiology	3	1			
First aid and safety		1		3	
Care and prevention of injuries	1	1		1	
Self-Care programs	1	2			
Consumer awareness	1			1	
Nutrition and weight control	1	2	1	2	1
Substance abuse	1	1	1		
Fitness program planning and improvement	1			5	
Fitness facilities and equipment		1	1	1	
Marketing of programs				1	2
Creating behavior changes					3
Physical testing and evaluation			1	1	1
Developmental exercise prescriptions			1	1	1
Administration				3	
Educational/professional behaviors	1	1		2	2

[a]Cognitive levels are taken from Bloom's (1956) *Taxonomy of Educational Objectives*.
[b]Numbers = number of test items for each subject area and each cognitive level.
Source: Dalton, 1989. Reproduced by permission.

**Figure 1. Test Design for General Studies Courses
in Philosophy and Religion.**

Views of the World

	Cognitive	Ethical	Religious
Developmental Processes			
Egocentrism	4[a]	4	4
Ethnocentrism	4	4	4
Global Reasoning	4	4	4

[a]Numbers = number of test items.
Source: O'Meara and Erwin, 1990.

world (cognitive, ethical, and religious) are specified. On the test, a problem is posed to the student, such as whether a woman awaiting execution, after having been convicted of exercising too much freedom of speech and freedom of inquiry, should escape—a situation much like Socrates' dilemma in *The Crito*. Statements are then presented to the student for assignment of importance:

- No one should give advice in this situation, because this woman's decision should be her own (egocentrism, or self-centered reasoning).
- This woman should consider the decisions of her friends, who want her to continue living (ethnocentrism, or reasoning centered in local communities or groups).
- This woman believes that a life without freedom is not worth living (global reasoning, or universal reasoning and valuing).

Subscales or scores are reported for egocentrism, ethnocentrism, and global reasoning, with twelve statements for each subscale. Problems are written from a cognitive, an ethical, or a religious point of view.

Writing Multiple-Choice Items. The writing of multiple-choice or similar recognition types of test items is an activity with which most educators are familiar. Multiple-choice tests cover a wider array of subject matter content than essay tests, but they require more time to construct. Wesman (1971, pp. 102–105) has an excellent chapter about the writing of test items, including multiple-choice items. Here are a few of his suggestions:

1.   Express the item as clearly as possible.
2.   Include all qualifications needed to provide a reasonable basis for response selection.
3.   Avoid nonfunctional words.
4.   Avoid unnecessary specificity in the test item's stem or responses.
5.   Be as accurate as possible in all parts of the test item.
6.   Adapt the level of difficulty to the group and purpose for which the test is intended.

A number of other writers have provided detailed descriptions about writing selected- or constructed-response items (Coffman, 1971; Conoley and O'Neil, 1979; Ebel, 1979; Gronlund, 1968; Miller, Williams, and Haladyna, 1978; Roid, 1979; Roid and Haladyna, 1982). Among other examples and hints, these writers suggest that "foils" or "distractors"—that is, the incorrect answers in selected-response formats—should be parallel in length, grammatical structure, and credibility. They also recommend that the following practices be avoided: (1) writing negative statements, particularly double negatives, which can be unnecessarily confusing; (2) using "all of the above" or "none of the above" as options; and (3) including specific determiners, such as "never" or "absolutely," which are seldom correct.

One of the main problems with selected-response test formats is determining how many answers the student chose by guessing. For example, with a 100-item multiple-choice test, if four response alternatives are available for each item, then a person should get at least 25 percent (one of four) of the items correct just by guessing.

Designing Constructed-Response Measures

Various types of performances and products have been outlined earlier. The challenge of assessing these stimuli is a new one for most faculty, who commonly employ multiple-choice and essay questions. To assess performances or products, two techniques are typically used: rating scales and checklists. A _rating scale_ consists of a series of items or statements that describe an aspect of a skill or a personal trait. For each rating item, the rater selects a category, from a continuum ranging from poor to good, that best fits the individual whose trait or skill is being measured. Various types of rating scales will be discussed later in the chapter. A _checklist_ is also composed of a series of observable behaviors indicative of a successful performance or product. These behaviors either are exhibited by the student or they are not. They are marked as either present or absent. In some assessment programs, such as that of Alverno College (Mentkowski and Doherty, 1984; Mentkowski and Loacker, 1985), these behaviors are called criteria. If the designated criteria are met or observed, then the competency, skill, or goal is mastered or passed. Flanagan (1954) referred to checklists as "critical incidents" of behavior that distinguish between effective and ineffective work. These behaviors may be demonstrated through written records, such as a diary or log; from machine records, such as a microcomputer; or from direct observation. The records may be obtained unobtrusively, as was described in Chapter Four, or actively through naturalistic or simulated settings (Frederiksen, 1965).

Checklists are preferable to rating scales when the presence or absence of a set or sequence of observable behaviors is important. These checklists contain a few consequential behaviors of a performance or product and more detailed descriptions of behaviors, similar to a rating scale (Geis, 1970; Roid and Haladyna, 1982). The checklist is a simpler measurement and therefore can be less diagnostic than a rating scale; however, some performances or products lend themselves to all-or-nothing components.

Problems with Rating Scales and Checklists. Any assessment method has unique advantages and disadvantages associated with it, and ratings are no exception. Roid and Haladyna (1982) specify four main problems with rating scales and checklists: lack of rater agreement, difficulty of construction and use, difficulty in defining the trait or construct, and raters' biases (pp. 70–71). Using the ratings of essays as an example, most researchers (Coffman, 1971; Finlayson, 1951; Hakel, 1982; Hartog and Rhodes, 1936; Pearson, 1955; Vernon and Millican, 1954) have focused on the problems of rater bias and disagreement. Their research may be summarized as follows: (1) Different raters tend to assign different ratings to the same student behavior. (2) A single rater tends to assign different ratings to the same student behavior or assessment product on different occasions. (3) The differences in ratings tend to increase when the assessment task asked of students is less structured (Coffman, 1971, p. 277; Anastasi, 1988). As noted in Chapter Four, these problems result in poor reliability, or low inter- or intrarater reliability.

The differences in ratings described are generally reflected in the following types of rater errors: (1) the error of severity, or rating too strictly; (2) the error of leniency, or rating too kindly; (3) the error of central tendency, or avoiding extreme judgments and giving ratings in the middle of a scale; and (4) the halo effect, or rating with bias, letting an overall opinion of the person influence one's specific ratings. Most of these errors can be prevented if raters are trained in the use of the rating scale and if the rating scale uses behavioral descriptors.

Difficulty in constructing and using a rating scale or checklist prevents many educators from using performance or products as assessment stimuli. Not only does it take a considerable length of time to design a comprehensive, well-described rating scale; it also takes a considerable commitment to observe the performance and sometimes the product. For example, viewing an artistic performance may consume more than two hours of time per student.

Difficulty in defining and judging what is to be measured remains a problem in the rating of a performance, product, or social-personal dimension. Often, the components or traits are abstract and do not lend themselves to concrete behaviors or definitive description. The rating scale may become vague and confusing to use. However, careful and precise definitional work can make excellent rating scales possible. Incidentally, the discussions that flow from faculty or staff deliberations about a rating scale's content often produce changes in curriculum or programs.

Constructed responses are typically furnished by the student in either written or oral form. Although constructed-response items seek to eliminate guessing, because there is nothing from which to choose, the meaning of a student's responses may be confounded with that student's general writing or speaking skills. For example, in an interview, a highly verbal student can produce a deceptively adequate answer.

Suggestions for Reducing Problems with Rating Scales and Checklists. To counter the various problems described, educators can take the following steps: (1) More than one observer should rate the students, and these observers or raters should have sufficient opportunity to view the students' work. (2) Students can be required to complete more than one performance or product. An art student, for example, can submit a painting, a sculpture, and a craft; a student nurse can be observed as he or she treats a variety of patients. (3) The rating sheet should cover a variety of aspects or components of the performance or behavior; that is, more than just one or two rating items should be used for evaluations. (4) The rating scale should contain only about three to seven reference points (or categories) per rating or checklist item. Raters are rarely able to discriminate more than seven categories, and reliability does not improve beyond this point either. Moreover, each reference point should be clearly defined in behavioral terms, including, for instance, elements of duration, intensity, or frequency of occurrence (O'Leary and Johnson, 1979).

Smode, Gruber, and Ely (1962, p. 46) outlined seven aspects of performance measures that can be reflected in the components of rating scales:

1. Time—for example, how long does it take a hygienist student to fluoride teeth?
2. Accuracy—to what degree is the student's solution correct for a given problem?
3. Frequency of occurrence—how often does the student social worker exhibit distracting behaviors while in therapy with a client?
4. Amount achieved or accomplished—how much money has a student "earned" in a simulated business portfolio of investments?

5.   Consumption or quantity used—how much of a chemical com-
      pound remains in a solution in a given chemical experiment?
6.   Behavior—when members of a group are presented with a
      problem to solve, such as in a case study, how able is each
      member to (1) define the problem, (2) suggest alternatives, and
      (3) help resolve conflicts?
7.   Condition or state of the individual in relation to the task—
      when presented with multicultural diversity, how tolerant is
      the student?

Categories 1 through 5 elicit frequency counts or amounts. Categories 6 and 7, more common categories for rating scales, call for more
subjective judgments.

    Stiggins (1987, p. 39) discusses several ways to increase the
reliability and validity of rating scales. To increase reliability of
assessments, (1) use clear criteria on the scale; (2) train raters to
minimize errors of leniency, central tendency, severity, and halo
bias; and (3) provide uniform conditions, stimuli, or settings in
which to elicit behaviors for rating. To increase validity, (1) be clear
about the purpose of the assessment; (2) define clearly the characteristics and levels of performance along appropriate continuums;
(3) arrange assessment exercises that sample the range of performance contexts; and (4) compare ratings with other available
evidence.

    Types of Rating Scales. Rating scales include three basic
types: *behaviorally anchored, semantic differential,* and *Likert.* Although the discussion that follows focuses on rating scales as observational assessments, these rating scale types apply equally well
to surveys and most self-report methods. *Behaviorally anchored
scales* are the most descriptive of the three types and the hardest to
design. As their name suggests, each area or concept to be rated
contains a series of possible behaviors, ranging from descriptions of
a poor performance or product to those of a superior performance
or product. In between are several levels of behavioral descriptors
or anchors, with each level representing a progressively higher degree of performance. Many rating sheets will just ask the rater to
mark a 1, 2, 3, or 4 for each rating item. But raters may not know

what a 1 means or how to distinguish between a 3 and a 4. When behavioral descriptions are attached to the numbers, the raters can more consistently ascribe a rating category.

Behaviorally anchored rating scales are a version of what is called analytical rating. That is, within a given ability, such as writing ability, there are several attributes or qualities to be rated: organization of content, sentence clarity, development of ideas, coherence, mechanical accuracy, and so on. Analytical ratings can be contrasted with holistic ratings, which many faculty have used in grading the Educational Testing Service's Advanced Placement Program examinations for high school students. Holistic ratings give an overall score, in a range such as 1 to 5, representing the overall ability of the student. Holistic ratings are valuable for certifying overall competence, but analytical ratings are more useful for diagnostic feedback. A holistic rating scale is shown as Resource A at the back of this book.

Semantic differential ratings (Osgood, Suci, and Tannenbaum, 1957) also contain a series of items, but each concept is bounded by bipolar adjectives representing contrasting views of the performance or product. For instance, consider the following rating stem:

Rate the student's ability to establish rapport with the client:

responsive : ___ : ___ : ___ : ___ : ___ : ___ : reserved

The adjectives represent bipolar opposites, with six categories or gradients as choices for rating the student's degree of "responsiveness" or "reservedness" in oral communication skills. The number of gradients or options between the adjectives depends on the raters' ability to discriminate among the choices. The greater the number of options from which to rate, the more difficult it is for the raters to choose and agree on the option. As mentioned, no more than seven options should be used. The semantic differential is not as descriptive as the behaviorally anchored rating scale because only two categories are listed.

Likert-scale ratings (Likert, 1932) list a stimulus statement or content item, to which the respondent marks "strongly agree," "slightly agree," "slightly disagree," or "strongly disagree." Variations of the response alternatives—such as "very rarely" to "almost always" or "not at all true of me" to "very true of me"—are made to suit the stimulus statement. Numerical values or weights are assigned to each response alternative and then summed across all items for a total score. These weights, for example, might be 1 for "strongly agree," 2 for "slightly agree," 4 for "slightly disagree," and 5 for "strongly disagree." The weights depend on the distance the educator believes to exist between the Likert response alternatives.

Advantages of the Likert type of rating scale include its simplicity and ease of construction and use. One disadvantage involves possible misinterpretation of the response options; for instance, "slightly agree" may mean different things to different raters (Fiske, 1981). In addition, the response options are not tailored to each stimulus statement or content item in the way that behaviorally anchored ratings are; consequently, some precision is lost. A last disadvantage concerns the tendency of some people to self-report only socially desirable characteristics or attitudes. Although this tendency does not present as great a problem as was first believed (Hogan and Nicholson, 1988), it should be considered nevertheless when one is constructing and analyzing stimulus statements. For example, Rest (1987) included a separate subscore for meaningless responses in his Defining Issues Test, a measure of moral development. The data of respondents who score high on this subscore are rejected as invalid.

Steps in Constructing Rating Scales and Checklists. Fogli, Hulin, and Blood (1971) and Priestley (1982) suggest that test designers follow these specific steps in constructing a rating scale:

1. Decide on the performance, process, product, or social-personal trait to be rated. For example, one may wish to assess writing abilities shown in a sample essay about "Steps for Finding a Job After Graduation."
2. Determine the various attributes or qualities of the performance, process, product, or trait to be rated.
3. List the important or critical areas, behaviors, characteristics, or aspects of the attribute or quality in step 2.

4. List the least important or undesirable areas, behaviors, characteristics, or aspects of each attribute or quality in step 2.
5. Decide on the type of rating scale for each aspect: Likert, semantic differential, or behaviorally anchored.
6. Form scales from the behaviors or characteristics described in steps 3 and 4 according to the type of rating scale. Use observable behaviors or characteristics.
7. For the behaviorally anchored type, the desirable and undesirable characteristics would be organized as optional categories for possible selection by each attribute quality. For the writing scale example, there are six optional gradients ranging from least to most desirable. In the semantic differential, only descriptions of the bipolar opposites are given. For the Likert, declarative statements are written for the desirable and undesirable characteristics listed in steps 3 and 4.
8. Write the directions for administering or assigning the assessment performance or product.
9. Write the directions for rating or scoring.
10. If this was not already done above, design or select the specific stimulus or task to be rated.
11. Pilot the scales and revise them as needed.

Steps in constructing a checklist include the following (see Geis, 1970; TenBrink, 1974):

1. Identify the performance, process, product, or social-personal trait relevant to your purpose.
2. List the important behaviors and characteristics in the sequence a skilled expert or highly developed person would exhibit.
3. List major errors or weak behaviors.
4. Write the directions for scoring.
5. Pilot with an expert and a typical student.
6. Revise the checklist from feedback received.

Surveys. Surveys, another common method for collecting assessment information, can elicit valuable information beyond the information obtained through rating scales and checklists. Although surveys are used for entering and exiting students, they are more commonly used for alumni follow-up. Such questionnaires pose statements about continuing education, employment history, and general perceptions about the programs and activities of the institution. An example of an institutionally constructed alumni survey is provided as Resource B at the back of this book. If a local survey is constructed, both academic and student affairs staff will want to participate in the construction, in order to gain feedback about their academic and student life programs. Standardized questionnaires and scoring services are available from the National Center for Higher Education Management Systems, the Educational Testing Service, and the American College Testing Program.

Besides general perceptions about the institution, individual academic departments may wish to add extra questions unique to students who majored in their program. What courses or aspects of their education have been particularly useful to them as alumni? What courses need to be added or improved? Such two-part alumni surveys furnish feedback about the institution as a whole and about an academic program.

Surveys or questionnaires are usually either factual (requesting behavioral or demographic information) or attitudinal (requesting perceptions about people or events). In factual surveys, questions are relatively straightforward, seeking direct answers. For instance, alumni surveys commonly request statements about employment history and continuing education. The alumni respond to these statements by listing the desired information or by checking a category from several options.

Attitudinal or satisfaction questionnaires describe or analyze the attitudes of a group of students or their degree of satisfaction with their education. Responses are self-rated by the student, typically on a Likert scale, such as "strongly agree," "slightly agree," "slightly disagree," and "strongly disagree." Statements should be written to reflect an attitude or a construct, and the rules previously specified for reliability and construct validity should be adhered to.

Peter Ewell reminds us that attitudinal questions may be framed as attributive self-ratings, such as "I have many doubts about what I am going to do with my life." Observational reports such as "I was encouraged to ask questions in class" also are common. Questions also may be posed as facts: "On the average, how often do you use the library resources?"

Aulepp and Delworth (1976, 1978) extended the use of Likert types of statements with what they called environmental referents. Consider the following example:

My adviser discusses career options for my major.   Strongly agree, slightly agree, slightly disagree, strongly disagree.

What things exist or have happened to make you feel this way?

What would you recommend be changed to improve the situation or what things should remain unchanged?

In the first statement, an attitude or a perception is categorized. With the two follow-up open-ended questions, more specific information is solicited about why these feelings exist and what might be changed.

Surveys are also useful when educators want to collect information about the student's involvement in campus activities. Institutions with active student life programs should consider recording the type and degree of participation in various student organizations. Resource C is a form used at James Madison University. The environmental content categories are campus events, such as plays or debates; sports; and academic experiences, employment, and community service. In each content category, questions are used to reveal the degree of participation for that particular activity. This dimension of involvement is based on Astin's (1984) study, which states that the amount of student learning and development from a program is proportional to the quantity and quality of student involvement in that program. For example, holding a leadership position produces greater benefits than merely being a member of a student organization.

Faculty may occasionally use questionnaires to assess students' involvement in activities related to the major. For instance, students' self-reports about type of library and computer usage provide worthwhile sources of information for comparing actual outcomes.

Developmental and attitudinal surveys often form the major

source of information about cognitive and affective developmental objectives. Self-perceptions, career development, ethics, and critical thinking are common developmental areas for assessment surveys.

Finally, surveys are used for the purpose of eliciting students' opinions about teaching. Braskamp, Brandenburg, and Orr (1984) have provided excellent examples and proper uses of such surveys. Although these questionnaires on student opinions of teaching are ubiquitous on college campuses, the information obtained is often supplemented with more direct assessment of students' learning and development.

Several tips about constructing questionnaires are given here (adapted from Mitchell and Jolley, 1988; Whitney, 1970).

1. Use simple words, avoiding technical jargon and ambiguous, equivocal, or unimportant questions.

2. Use words and terms that are already understood. For example, does "rate the student affairs program" mean "react to the counseling services," "to the residential programs," "to the student activities offices," or what? Does "rate your preparation for citizenship" mean the American history course, a lecture series, or something else?

3. Avoid personal questions—for instance, about salary levels or birth control use—unless they are necessary; if you must use them, place them at the end of the questionnaire. They arouse suspicion.

4. Make sure the students have the information you ask for. For example, alumni may furnish faulty information if they are asked to recall the value of particular courses taken twenty years earlier.

5. Ask questions that furnish a productive response, one that leads to action by the institution. For example, it may be interesting to know that 53 percent of the students voted for President Bush in the last election, but a question about voting behavior offers little information for educational programming purposes.

6. Focus on a single issue per statement. For example, avoid "The instructional and advising services prepared me for my

career." What is to be addressed? Preparation by the instructor *or* the advising services?

7. Avoid asking for information if it is available elsewhere, and avoid designing a lengthy form.

8. Create sufficient incentive for the student to respond, and live up to promises made to the students, such as providing a copy of the results.

9. Avoid questions that encourage a "favorable response" or questions that are loaded with social desirability. For example, avoid questions such as "Did you leave the institution with a highly developed sense of ethics?"

10. Avoid leading questions, such as "Do you approve of expanding the education degree program to five years?"

Questionnaires should not be administered unless the information will be used to improve an administrative or academic program. The proliferation of surveys on campuses can furnish interesting opinions but can also reduce students' seriousness about assessment unless they later see that the information has been put to good use.

Interviews. Before a questionnaire, rating scale, or checklist is designed, interviews are typically conducted so that educators can glean ideas about possible opinions of respondents. A few initial interviews can provide responses for the content of more efficient questionnaires. Interviewing allows the assessor to ask open-ended questions and to probe further with additional follow-up questions.

Informal interviews can be conversational, providing the student with only the broadest guidelines for responding. For example, "What did you learn in this program?" Standardized interviews are more structured processes. The interviewer not only asks more specific questions but also anticipates most responses with a previously designed checklist or rating scale. Informal interviews usually precede standardized interviews, to give a sample range of responses for framing the checklist or rating scale and to polish the directions and questions. Although the standardization may reduce student spontaneity, the increased structure minimizes interviewer bias by ensuring that each student receives the same questions.

Standardized interviews are typically employed, under the name of oral exams, for faculty assessing in the major or in liberal studies. As Colby, Kohlberg, Gibbs, and Lieberman's (1983) Moral Judgment Interview and Baxter-Magolda's (1987) Measure of Epistemological Reflection illustrate, structured interviews also can be used for assessing development.

Although most of us conceive of interviewing single students, the focused interview, formulated by Merton, Fiske, and Kendall (1956), draws together a homogeneous group of students in a group interview. Prompted by an interviewer's questions, the group members can play off each other's responses.

focus group (handwritten margin note)

Analyzing the Reliability of Assessment Data

There are two sets of techniques for analyzing the reliability of assessment data. The first set is called the elementary item analysis. This type of analysis helps educators improve the internal consistency of norm-referenced interpretations. Elementary item analysis is typically used with assessment formats that have right or wrong answers, such as multiple-choice tests, or with partial credit scales, such as Likert or semantic differential scales. The second, more sophisticated set of techniques is based on generalizability measurement theory. This theory enables educators to determine reliability for criterion-referenced approaches and to diagnose different sources of error or unreliability.

Elementary item analysis allows the examination of a number of important questions. A test item's difficulty can be determined, to ensure that it is appropriate for the type of test being used. The relationship between high scores on the instrument as a whole and correct answers to a particular test item can be found, so that test items that do not contribute to the test's reliability can be eliminated. For criterion-referenced interpretations, "instructional sensitivity" can be measured. Do students who have participated in the institution or program answer a particular question correctly more often than students who have not?

Elementary item analyses produce three numerical indices, which can be examined for each multiple-choice, Likert, or semantic differential test item: (1) the test item difficulty index, (2) the test item and total score correlation, and (3) the item discrimination index. The test item difficulty index simply represents the proportion or percentage of students answering the particular test item correctly. For a norm-referenced interpretation, test item difficulties should be around .5, or 50 percent correct. For a criterion-referenced framework, the item difficulties are usually higher than .5, depending on expected mastery or competency levels.

The second index, item-score correlation, is simply the relationship between getting a particular test item correct and the total item score. The item-score index is a correlation ranging from -1.0 to +1.0, with high values for a question indicating that students who answered that question correctly are also scoring high on the test itself.

The third index, the item discrimination index, includes two basic types. The first type is used with norm-referenced interpretations and is a measure of the difference between the proportion of students with high test scores answering the test item correctly and the proportion of students with low test scores answering the same test item correctly. High or low test scores are usually defined as the top 27 percent or the bottom 27 percent of the student group. Questions with negative discrimination differences may be problem questions, since low-scoring students were more likely to answer the test item correctly than high-scoring students. The second type of discrimination index is generally used with criterion-referenced interpretations and examines "instructional sensitivity," or the difference between students who have received instruction and students who have not (Crocker and Algina, 1986). Two measures of this index will be presented here. The first measure is the difference between the proportion of students who answered the particular test item correctly at the posttest, or after participating in the instruction or program, and the proportion of students who answered it correctly at the pretest, or before participation (Cox and Vargas, 1966). Expressed symbolically, the measure is $D = P_{POST} - P_{PRE}$.

The other instructional sensitivity measure, proposed by Brennan (1972), uses mastery or cutoff scores: $B = (U/n_1) - (L/n_2)$, where n_1 is the number scoring above the cutoff level, n_2 is the number scoring below, U is the number above the cutoff who answered the particular item correctly, and L is the number of students below the cutoff who answered the item correctly. This B value ranges from -1.0 to $+1.0$, with higher positive values sought for each item (Crocker and Algina, 1986, p. 330).

Most campus computing centers have software packages for calculating these numerical indices. For example, *Statistical Package for the Social Sciences, Version X* (SPSS, 1986), has a procedure called RELIABILITY, which is directly useful for Likert and semantic differential types and may be programmed for a multiple-choice type. *Statistical Analysis System* (SAS Institute, 1990) has a procedure called PROC CORR ALPHA (p. 214) for multiple-choice tests.

The more sophisticated item-analysis techniques, called item-response theory or latent-trait theory, examine item difficulty, item discrimination, and guessing factors simultaneously. See Crocker and Algina (1986), Hambleton (1983), and Traub and Wolf (1981) for further information.

Generalizability theory allows the designers of an assessment method to study various components, or facets, that may contribute to lack of reliability. For instance, suppose an art department asked students to submit portfolios of their artistic products for review. Several facets, or possible sources of error, can arise from such an assessment project. They may include the raters, the rating scale, the art object to be rated, and so on. For example, different raters may produce different ratings; the rating scale may be interpreted in different ways by the faculty; and different art objects, such as paintings, sculptures, and drawings, may furnish different perspectives of artistic ability. Generalizability information alerts the assessment designer as to which facet or source of error is a problem. Do the raters need additional training in the rating process? Does the rating scale need modification? Are the objects in the portfolio sufficient for judging artistic ability? Furthermore, generalizability theory allows one to study the precision of the assessment, given a designated cutoff score. In summary, generalizability information helps the designer determine the number of raters, the number of rating items, the criterion levels, and other such facets that can be varied. See Brennen (1983) for more detailed information.

Conclusion

This chapter has offered suggestions for designing one's own assessment methods. A distinction was made between selected- and constructed-response formats for students, and particular attention was given to mutiple-choice items, rating scales, checklists, surveys, and interviews. The next chapter focuses on strategies for collecting assessment information.

SIX

Collecting and Maintaining Information

Collecting and maintaining assessment information are complex processes. Collecting information is not the mere administration of a test to a group of willing undergraduates. It is a process of involving a variety of people in data collection and of deciding when data should be collected. Maintaining assessment information will pose problems as the amount of information grows. This chapter will discuss both the collection and the maintenance of assessment information, as well as the costs and staffing of an assessment program.

The premise behind assessment is that the information collected will be used to help educators make decisions about academic and student life programs. To what extent can assessment information be used in this decision-making process? How important is it to base decisions on empirical information? Evaluation of programs is a continuous process; the degree to which the administration of an institution desires empirical information for the decision-making process determines how much support will be devoted to an assessment program. If an administration envisions a minimal role for empirical information in the planning and operational functions of an institution, few resources will be allocated to the collection, analysis, and reporting of assessment information.

Sampling Issues

The questions "Whom do we assess?" and "When and how often do we assess?" are related to student sampling—that is, assessing a subgroup of an institution's students and then generalizing with confidence to the larger student population. In general, students are assessed as a cohort, a cohort being a group of students who share the same attribute. Typical cohorts are freshmen, students in the same student organization, or students majoring in the same field of study. Most cohorts are studied over time; assessment information is collected at orientation, at the middle of undergraduate studies, in the senior term, and at some designated point after graduation. Other cohorts may be assessed with regard to some special program in the campus environment, such as after participation in a student organization or after a learning-living experience in the residential halls.

Often, it is too inconvenient or expensive to assess every student at a medium- or large-sized institution. In such instances, educators may wish to select at random a small group of students who ideally would represent the characteristics of all the students in a given cohort. For example, if the freshman class consisted of 4,000 students, a systematic random sample of the freshmen whose identification numbers ended in 2 would produce a more moderate-sized group of 400 to assess. Of course, available demographic characteristics of the students who participate—characteristics such as gender, race or ethnic background, and grade point averages—should be compared with the demographic characteristics of students in the entire group or cohort.

Selecting a sample has a technical side. Mendenhall, Ott, and Scheaffer (1971) and Rossi, Wright, and Anderson (1983) present a more complex treatment of types of samples, such as systematic, stratified, and cluster, and accuracy indexes for the reader to pursue. Some rough guidelines will be presented here as an introduction. First, one must determine how large the universe of students is. Second, one must decide what confidence level and sampling are desired for the study. Table 6 lists sample sizes that can be drawn given the known size of the entire population or universe of students.

Table 6. Required Sample Size as a Function of Population Size, Desired Accuracy, and Level of Confidence.

Confidence Level:	95%	90%	85%	80%	95%	90%	85%	80%	95%	90%	85%	80%
Sampling Error:	5%	5%	5%	5%	3%	3%	3%	3%	1%	1%	1%	1%
Size of Universe												
50	44	42	40	39	48	47	46	45	50	50	50	49
100	79	73	167	63	92	88	85	82	99	99	98	98
200	132	116	102	92	169	159	148	140	196	194	193	191
500	217	178	147	126	343	302	268	242	476	466	456	447
1,000	278	216	172	145	521	434	365	319	907	873	838	809
2,000	322	242	188	156	705	554	447	380	1,661	1,550	1,443	1,357
5,000	357	261	199	163	894	664	516	429	3,311	2,897	2,545	2,290
10,000	370	268	203	166	982	711	545	448	4,950	4,079	3,414	2,970
20,000	377	272	205	168	1,033	737	560	459	6,578	5,124	4,117	3,488
50,000	381	274	207	168	1,066	754	569	465	8,195	6,055	4,697	3,896
100,000	383	275	207	169	1,077	760	573	467	8,926	6,445	4,929	4,054

Example of use of table: If you are sampling from a universe of fifty people and you want to have 90 percent confidence that your results will be within 5 percent of the true percentage in the population, you need to randomly sample forty-two people.

Source: David Van Amburg of David Van Amburg & Associates, Inc. Reproduced by permission.

Table 6 also lists sample sizes that are required for given confidence levels and sampling errors. Confidence level reflects the probability that the sample size approximates the characteristics of the universe. Sampling error reflects the probability that one's results will be within a certain percentage of the true results in the population.

If one is generalizing from a random sample to all undergraduates at the institution, then the universe or population is the total number of students at the institution. If one wishes to generalize to students within a college or within a class, then one must sample within that cluster or strata of interest. One cannot, for instance, base the sample on all undergraduates, collect the data, and then generalize to students in the business school. Initially, random samples should be drawn separately from within each college. Similarly, if one wishes to report results by educational level, then separate random samples should be selected within each of the freshman, sophomore, junior, and senior classes.

A last note of caution should be considered about random sampling. Assuming that one draws an appropriate random sample, all the students in that sample should participate if the confidence level and sampling errors are to be maintained. In practice, however, total turnout of a random sample of students rarely occurs. Sampling can also reduce the number of groups for comparison. For example, if too few students show up from a particular major, not enough student data are available to generalize about that major program. For these reasons, institutions ultimately choose not to sample.

Times for Collecting Information

A very convenient time to collect assessment information is during the orientation program for new students, before the students have been influenced by their attendance at the institution. During this period, baseline information can be readily obtained. That is, with the greater diversity of students today and their changing backgrounds, it is important to assess, not assume, students' entering levels of ability and development. Information about students' basic skills is routinely collected at matriculation, and much of this information is used for placement, remediation, and proficiency purposes. However, measures of general education, such as liberal arts knowledge or intellectual developmental level, are not widely assessed at entry. Some students may already possess the desired skill or trait and may not need a particular course or service, while most students will be learning or developing the skill or trait at the institution.

Often, assessment information is collected at the beginning of a program and used immediately for diagnostic purposes. Students are asked, for example, to perform musical auditions, submit an art portfolio at admissions time, and write autobiographical statements about their career goals. The assessment process may help in conducting these evaluations. For example, in some instances, a standard rating sheet may be constructed to document a previously less formal process of evaluation. This documentation usually provides clearer feedback for the student and furnishes a better baseline record of students' learning and development.

These students can be followed up with reassessment at a logical time, such as the end of the sophomore year. Depending on institutional requirements, measures of basic studies are often collected after the sophomore year, when most basic studies courses have been completed. Other institutions may wait until the end of the junior or senior year. Usually, the senior year is reserved for assessment activities in the major. Whatever periods are chosen, it is recommended that these periods be consistent, so that students can plan accordingly. Students generally respond well to retesting on general education measures if it is understood that their growth measures will be shared with them.

Assessment information may be collected through senior coursework, typically through a senior seminar or similar capstone experience. The practice of assessment has stimulated or resurrected the senior seminars, an occasion for the student to reflect on prior learning experiences and integrate them into a culminating experience. Assessment fits into this purpose by profiling the student's strengths and weaknesses in the major program of study. Most students find this feedback very beneficial at the end of their undergraduate studies. Assessment as a part of a capstone experience overcomes many problems of students' participation and motivation, since the purpose and the benefits of the senior assessment are clear to the students.

Assessment in this capstone course is taking different forms. Many colleges have reinstated comprehensive examinations for undergraduates. In certain programs, the assessment method is more active. The student produces a project or performs some act that encompasses a variety of knowledge and skills obtained from prior coursework. The various methods a department might consider were discussed in Chapters Three and Four.

Finally, assessment information can be obtained after the students have graduated. Proprietary and locally constructed questionnaires include queries about employment history, continuing education, and reflection on past educational experiences. Most of these contacts are through the mail; however, innovative approaches might produce other kinds of information. For instance, alumni offices could hold special homecoming gatherings for selected groups of students. Former band members could be polled about their continuing interest in music. Former students who participated in student organizations could be questioned about their continued participation in community or civic groups. Such contacts with alumni should not be tied to fund raising, nor should any assumptions be made about what the alumnus is doing now. It should not be assumed, for instance, that former student leaders are now community leaders.

Besides the follow-up of an educational class, other selected cohorts of students may be assessed because of their involvement or participation in a particular part of the campus environment. Certain cohorts of students may have something in common that other students do not. For example, does participation in student government enhance a student's development of autonomy? Students who participate in student government may be assessed as a separate cohort to study associated program impact. Similarly, honor students, athletes, campus leaders, debaters, actors, and so on may have benefited from these distinct experiences. An institution might study out-of-the-class experiences, documenting their contribution toward learning and development.

Patton (1987) has discussed the importance of probing small groups of students who are special cases, typical cases, or confirming and disconfirming cases, to name a few of his categories for specialized sampling. Extreme or deviant students may be individuals who scored at the very top or the very bottom of an assessment method. "Typical cases" refers to students who display the level of development characteristic of a certain time period—for example, the typical concerns about self or identity expressed by the one-month freshman. Confirming or disconfirming cases relate to new patterns or ideas. For instance, if a borderline student was allowed to take a usual course load although his or her placement test scores were marginally passing, how well has the student performed? Was the cutoff score appropriate?

Use of Microcomputers

A nontraditional method for collecting information, the use of microcomputers, will be discussed only briefly. With the advent of more powerful and less expensive computers, a new future of data collection and ongoing analysis is opening up. Although few examples currently exist, it is wise to anticipate that the computer will be used more frequently for data collection in the future. In some cases, the computer will simply replace paper-and-pencil methods of assessment. In more sophisticated applications, assessment exercises will be tailored to the individual student. Such assessment models will draw upon cognitive psychology, artificial intelligence, and item-response measurement theory to create instruments; instantly analyze responses; and then present another assessment exercise using information from prior exercises. Current models display multiple-choice items, one at a time; future assessment exercises will use graphics and audio effects to present more stimulating prompts. An example of an initial adaptive testing program is available from the College Board (1990) with its Computerized Placement Tests. The student's answers to earlier questions determine what later questions will be. In this way, a student's ability is more precisely measured in much less time.

Assessment Costs

As an institution considers whether to undertake, continue, or expand an assessment program, it will inevitably consider the benefits and costs of the program. Is assessment worth the benefits? Of course, for most institutions, the question is not whether assessment will exist but how large will the program be? Table 7 charts some of the benefits and costs of assessment.

Primary benefits may accrue from increased accountability to external agencies and increased effectiveness of students' learning and development. The loss of these benefits may lead to loss of accreditation, decreased enrollments and budgets (Lewis, 1988), or minimal learning and negative developmental experiences.

The costs of assessment will vary, of course, according to the size of the institution, the comprehensiveness of its assessment plan, and the degree of technical expertise available on campus. The size of the institution obviously affects the number of tests and the scoring and data storage costs. The comprehensiveness of the assessment plan is also a major determinant of costs. Does the institution's assessment program encompass both student and academic affairs? Will the assessment program feed information back to individual students? This is a fairly labor-intensive activity. Are the assessment methods restricted to nationally designed multiple-choice examinations, or will academic and student affairs departments use other methods, such as ratings of assessment performance, processes, or products? Such methods can be lengthy to observe, time consuming to rate, and expensive to monitor and tabulate.

Ewell and Jones (1985) have written a summary of assessment costs for a small, private liberal arts college; a public research university; a regional comprehensive university; and a community college. Their report includes estimates of test and proctor costs, as well as the cost of hiring a measurement specialist to coordinate the program and analyze assessment information.

Institutions either use existing personnel or hire assessment specialists to oversee assessment programs. These assessment specialists should have not only a background in statistics but also strong measurement skills for tests and rating scale construction. Computing skills are necessary, and a knowledge of student development assessment methods is helpful. Assessment specialists who have these skills are a valuable commodity now, with their average starting salaries still rising. A separate assessment specialist might be needed for institutions with a strong developmental orientation

Table 7. Costs and Benefits of Assessment in Higher Education: Who Benefits and Who Bears the Burden?

Costs and Benefits of Evaluation	Perspectives			
	Staff[a]	Institution[b]	Students[c]	Society[d]
Costs				
Direct Resource Costs				
Personnel and consultants		–		–
Facilities and equipment		–		–
Supplies and materials		–		–
Travel and data processing		–		–
Incidental and Opportunity Costs				
Possible diminished morale/collegiality	–	–	–	
Possible legal and moral burdens	–	–		–
Possible misinformation		–	–	–
Opportunity costs of student time		–	–	
Opportunity costs of staff time	–			–
Opportunity costs of monitoring	–			
Benefits				
Direct Information Benefits				
Improved accountability	+/–	+/–	+	+
Improved effectiveness	+	+	+	+
Improved efficiency	+/–	+	+	+
Incidental and Secondary Benefits				
Incidental student learning			+	+
Incidental changes in staff attitudes	+/–	+/–	+/–	
Incidental knowledge production	+/–	+/–	+/–	+
New/declined accreditation	+/–	+/–	+/–	+
Increased/decreased quality of students	+/–	+/–	+/–	
Increased/decreased external resources	+/–	+/–	+/–	–/+

[a]Faculty and administration in program evaluated.
[b]Other institutional faculty and staff, including administration, overseers, and evaluators.
[c]Viewed as sole consumers of institutional product.
[d]Includes donors, government agencies, legislatures, foundations, parents, and alumni.
Source: Reprinted from Lewis, 1988, p. 72.

in student affairs. Focusing on developmental outcome assessment, this person should have a background in cognitive and affective developmental theory and measurement.

Many institutions use an existing testing center, institutional research office, or academic planning group for coordination of assessment (Ewell and Jones, 1985). Research in these offices has traditionally included summary studies reporting data about the number of full-time-student equivalents and space allocation figures. Assessment data are different because they require measures about the quality of the data; that is, their reliability and validity. Information about the square feet of classroom space does not contain the measurement error characteristic of a locally designed test about critical thinking. In addition, some institutional research offices that do not report to academic or student affairs are now reporting to vice presidents who have direct vested interests in program improvement or accountability. However, many traditional testing centers and institutional research offices are responding to the new needs of assessment by hiring new staff or establishing staff development training programs. National organizations such as the American Association for Higher Education, Measurement Services Association of the National Council for Measurement in Education, and the Association for Institutional Research now devote part of their national meetings to presentations about outcome assessment in higher education.

Various attempts have been made to determine the cost of assessment and evaluation (Lewis, 1988), but costs have proved "difficult, if not impossible" to establish (Alkin and Ruskus, 1984, p. 12). Guidelines range from 1 to 3 percent of a total program's cost (Bowen, 1985) to 10 percent (Joint Committee on Standards for Educational Evaluation, 1981). In actuality, few of the most successful assessment programs in higher education reach one-half of 1 percent of an institution's total budget.

The greatest problem for funding has to do with released time for faculty and staff. For instance, if a faculty member serves as assessment coordinator for an assessment in the major project, should that faculty member be released from other duties? This issue is a particular sticking point because of the newness of the practice and the amount of money involved. The salary of an institutional assessment coordinator and test-leasing costs are easier to accept as needed costs. Until assessment becomes a more accepted practice in higher education, allocation of funds will be slow to come.

Maintaining Assessment Information

The collection of assessment information leads to another step in the assessment process, that of storing and maintaining assessment information. Assessment information will need to be stored for later distribution and use. In addition, the data stored can be compared with data that are collected later. Computerized student information systems now enable institutions to store assessment data by individual student. Several years ago, proprietary software vendors, such as Information Associates and Systems and Computer Technology, designed data-base systems especially for higher education. These systems were created to store demographic, admissions, transcript, financial aid, and accounts payable information. This information was pooled into a single data base, to reduce duplication of the same element of information in more than one office or department. Updating such common information could then be reflected in every campus office at the same time. In addition, authorized persons could view needed information from other offices. For example, a faculty member could view a student's transcript to assist in advising. A student affairs person might need to check on a student's financial aid status. Most of the information was recorded and maintained to support the operations of the institution; thus, the name "management information system" (MIS) became popular. Because these systems tended to concentrate on storage efficiencies rather than staff needs, new "decision support systems" were developed (Beeler, 1989). These systems coupled data with analytical and reporting types of software, which organize and present information in a form to meet the administrator's need for student information (Kroenke and Dolan, 1987). The National Center for Higher Education Management Systems (Ewell, Parker, and Jones, 1988) has also pioneered the use of longitudinal student-tracking systems. Tracking systems organize student data in ways that promote institutional effectiveness. The collection of additional student assessment information calls for a different yet overlapping application of data-base systems: the availability of learning and developing information to promote student growth (Erwin and Miller, 1985; Erwin and Tollefson, 1982).

Such student computerized information systems lend themselves well to storing and displaying student assessment data. Existing management information systems could be modified at many institutions to include another segment or file of information containing scores or ratings from any departmental or institution-wide assessment effort. Assessment information collected at entry, such as basic skills test scores, pretest measures of general education, or pretest measures from the major might be stored for later analyses with sophomore or senior measures. Just like any other piece of information stored in a data-base system, test scores or ratings could be restricted for viewing to authorized staff. For instance, scores from the Educational Testing Service's (1988) Major Field Achievement Test in political science could be restricted only to political science faculty. Data can be stored throughout the student's undergraduate years and thereafter if so desired. For example, it is useful to compare outcome measures collected during the undergraduate years to behaviors reported from the alumni.

The availability of information about students' learning and development opens up opportunities not only to work individually with students on a more informed basis but also to study patterns of student behavior among the variety of stored data. Authorized faculty advisers and designated student affairs staff might be better-informed advisers and counselors if they have access at a computer terminal to learning and development measures. Coursework and participation in student services might be recommended on the basis of assessment data. In addition, authorized educators may retrieve certain outcome measures for comparison with other student measures of involvement in the campus environment. For instance, course grades and course selection patterns could be compared with liberal studies assessment scores or ratings. Is living in the residence halls associated with higher psychosocial development measures? Are students at risk being placed in initial freshman coursework according to their abilities? The possibilities for study of students' learning and development are limited only by the information stored in the system and by the creativity of the educator involved. Erwin and Tollefson (1982) provide a more detailed model for design and use of computerized data-base systems for student development.

Conclusion

This chapter addressed strategies for collecting and maintaining assessment information. Issues about how many students to assess, when to assess them, and what cost factors to consider were discussed. Issues were also raised about electronic maintenance of the information because of the volume and length of time for maintaining it. (Chapter Eight discusses in detail oversight and responsibility to ensure the proper use of confidential information.)

SEVEN

Analyzing Information and Drawing Conclusions

 Analysis is the process of aggregating, usually in quantitative form, students' responses to various assessment stimuli, and of describing the overall characteristics, patterns, and parts of these student data to obtain answers to questions. Interpreting is describing in narrative form what the analyses mean in relation to questions of interest and the program at hand. Analyses are often conducted with the help of an assessment person, a measurement specialist, or a statistician. Interpretation is generally the major responsibility of the persons whose programs are under study. In other words, persons with training in assessment may help in describing statistical patterns and differences, but faculty or student affairs staff should be heavily involved in interpreting any conclusions about their respective programs.

Are the collected data worth analyzing? Methods for determining the quality of the assessment information have already been mentioned in discussions about reliability, validity, and sampling. If these standards for quality of information are not met, it may not be wise to continue analyzing what the data mean. If the reliability, however defined, of the data is poor, any conclusions about the quality of the designated program are also suspect. If the instruments are not relevant, representative, and valid for the program, the data collected will be misleading and faulty. If the sampling procedures are spotty, any interpretations about the available data are also risky. For example, if there was a low turnout of graduating seniors or a poor response rate on a survey, educators will be unable to make generalizations about the effects of a program. If in spite of these defects, faculties or staffs believe that the data are still worth analyzing, they should use extreme caution in drawing any conclusions.

Chapter Five covered several techniques for determining how reliable and how valid one's scores or ratings are. This chapter will deal primarily with the analysis of assessment scores or ratings. Because educators and their constituents analyze assessment scores and ratings against perceived standards, the first part of the chapter will deal with the setting of standards or cutoff scores. Did the students do well on the test? Determining "well" is often not as simple as it might intuitively seem. The later part of the chapter will cover several models for aggregating and analyzing the assessment information. Why do some students score or rate higher than other students? Why do some groups of students learn or develop more than other groups of students? What types of educational experiences make a difference in students' learning and development? What aspects of the campus environment are associated with students' learning and development?

Brinkerhoff, Brethower, Hluchkyj, and Nowakowski (1983) offer the following guidelines for the process of data analysis and interpretation:

1. Review the questions to be addressed. What does one seek to know from the assessment study?
2. Prepare basic descriptive analyses.
3. Select the appropriate analytical model for the available data, distinguishing between the outcome measures and the measures of the environmental program that purports to influence these outcomes.
4. Given the limitations of the model, analyze the basic issues, trends, and relationships among the measures of interest.
5. Noting the limitations of the analyses, interpret the findings.

In the initial assessment step, establishing program objectives, questions commonly arise about the quality of several aspects of the program. As was noted earlier, the search for evidence about these questions leads faculty and staff to the most valuable part of assessment. After data have been collected, have these questions changed? Do other questions need to be added? Are students learning according to faculty's expectations?

Some descriptive analyses may have already been prepared through reliability studies and survey returns. In addition, what are the basic frequencies of students' responses to various instruments? What are the averages and other measures of central tendency? What are the ranges of scores and other measures of dispersion? What are the percentile ranks for norm-referenced instruments?

Analyses of issues and relationships (discussed later in this chapter) should also be guided by the initial questions of concern. Also, is the evidence of sufficient strength, both in the quality of the information and in the quality of analyses, to warrant the drawing of conclusions? In programs with a small number of graduates, several years of data may need to be compiled before any conclusions can be drawn. In most cases, the answering of some questions usually leads to the formulation of additional questions. Finally, people who deliver the service should take the major responsibility in the interpretation of the findings.

Setting Performance or Competency Levels

How many students did well or rated well on the assessment test? How many students learned what was intended? Who performed above the desired level or criterion? How many passed the test? These are questions posed by educators in the instructional unit as well as by officials outside the institution. Their purposes for asking may be different; nevertheless, it is natural to want to know whether standards have been met. Standards denote quality, and quality education is everyone's aim. How many times has one heard about the problem of grade inflation, and who does not have a personal desire for standards (Shepard, 1980)? The initial questions in the analysis stage often gravitate to the issue of standards. And whenever standards are mentioned, the issue at hand for faculty and administrators is how standards should be established.

To state the problem another way, how should the criterion

level be set? What is the cutoff score or rating level that denotes competence in a discipline? Given a locally designed test or a standardized test from a testing organization, how do faculty members determine the level of competency for their students? Arbitrarily selecting a cutoff level of 60 percent might work for a classroom test, but something more defensible is called for in an end-of-the-program measure.

Determining a level of competency is an important aspect of assessment because the value of final classification decisions may rest on this level as much as on the validity of the assessment method itself (Shepard, 1980). The assessment method can effectively mirror the content of the program under study; however, where the cutoff level is drawn determines how many students actually benefited from the program. As necessary as it appears to use standards, it is equally difficult to determine them. Shepard (1980) claims that standard setting imposes an artificial dichotomy. Extreme groups of students can be identified as excellent or incompetent, but what about the middle group? Some educational objectives, such as skills, lend themselves well to a dichotomy; one can demonstrate the skill or one cannot. Other educational objectives of learning and development are more continuous in nature. What one knows or feels is a matter of degree in the measurement.

Realistically, there is no error-free approach to setting a level of mastery for any assessment instruments. Invariably, a student will score below the cutoff level and yet will truly know the material. On the other hand, some students who do not know the material will pass the particular assessment test because the cutoff score was set too low. After a trial exercise, many educators will find that the initial cutoff score or rating level needs adjusting to account for too high or too low expectations. Most faculty set the cutoff level too high initially, often having unrealistic expectations for their students.

Setting a mastery or competence level for rating scales is sometimes easier than setting one for multiple-choice tests. Rating scales provide clearer behavior descriptions of the desired outcome. Consider the following examples from one item of a behaviorally anchored rating scale about interpersonal communication skills:

Rate the student interviewer's involvement with the interviewee on a personal level:

4. Works to establish rapport. Communicates freely and openly, shows interest and adapts style to fit group needs. Able to work with different types of personalities in order to facilitate communication.
3. Appears detached and distant during interactions. Has difficulty maintaining flow of information from the group.
2. Overly eager to please the group and its members. Too casual so that the point of the meeting is often lost.
1. Positive communication in most cases but some difficulty adapting to different types of personalities.

Simple percentages of students categorized in the four skill levels furnish information about the level of functioning. Faculty or student affairs staff would choose their expectations among the four levels according to the purposes of their program. Other rating scale examples are given in Chapter Five.

Essentially, three broad classes of standard setting for selected-response formats, such as multiple-choice tests, are used: judgments based on holistic impressions; judgments based on review of test items, or content; and judgments based on students' test results (Crocker and Algina, 1986, p. 411; Shepard, 1980). The cutoff level corresponds to the percentage of test items a student with a minimum level of competency should answer correctly. Faculty should be cautioned that this level is a minimum competency level, not a level attained by typical *B* students. Of course, a higher cutoff standard could be designated for excellent students; however, the typical focus is on minimum competency for graduates in the major or basic studies. For judgments based on holistic impressions, a number of expert judges are polled and the levels they set are averaged. The expert judges will usually be departmental faculty, with one or more outside reviewers in the same discipline brought in as consultants (Crocker and Algina, 1986). It is important that the rating group include several judges. To build credibility for the standards, departments may wish to include persons outside their department and outside the institution. Institutions concerned about the acceptance of their standards of quality are wise to include other persons representing several constituencies. The inclusion of educators in the discipline at other institutions, professionals in the field, accreditation officials, and governmental officials strengthens any conclusions drawn. A problem with this method occurs because different judges have different areas of expertise and, therefore, might place different emphases, which would result in fluctuating standards from judge to judge (Crocker and Algina, 1986).

A second approach to standard setting involves judgments made about the content of assessment methods. In particular, this method for standard setting entails reviewing each test item separately and rating its importance. Several procedures for reviewing test content are available (see Angoff, 1971; Ebel, 1979; Jaeger, 1978; Martenza, 1977; and Nedelsky, 1954). In Angoff's procedure, each judge reviews each test item and assigns a probability that a minimally competent student will answer it correctly. Again, the judge, especially the faculty member, must imagine the lowest C or perhaps a D student in these judgments. Martenza's approach includes the following steps: (1) The judge reviews each test item and rates its importance for the minimally competent graduate in the program. (2) The judge awards from one to ten points for each test item, with ten points being "extremely important" and one point, "of little importance." For example:

Test Item Number	Importance
1	10
2	5
3	1
4	8
5	6
	30

(3) The "importance" ratings for all the test items are totaled (the total in the example is 30); this figure is divided by the total number of test items ($30/5 = 6$), and the resulting figure is multiplied by 10 (6 times $10 = 60$) to obtain the percent. Consequently, for this example, a single student would need to score at least 60 percent correct in order to reach minimum competency of this five-item test (Martenza, 1977, p. 270).

Ebel (1979) used a modification of this approach by including also a weight not only for the importance of item content but also for the difficulty of the test item. Angoff's (1971) and Martenza's (1977) procedures assume that each test item is of equal difficulty, an unlikely assumption. In Ebel's technique, judges sort the test items on a chart containing three levels of difficulty (difficult, medium, or easy) and four levels of relevance (essential, important, acceptable, or questionable). Each cell is awarded a level of probability of success. For example, easy-essential items would be assigned a 90% probability of success. In practice, the two dimensions of difficulty and relevance are confused by judges (Shepard, 1980). Further details about guessing or item difficulty are provided by Millman (1973, 1974), Hambleton, Swaminathan, Algina, and Coulson (1978), and Novick and Lewis (1974).

The primary disadvantages of judging test content are that judges tend to disagree and to omit item ratings if the item is outside their area of expertise. Because their reviews are hypothetical, their expectations can also be unrealistic. That is why some people prefer a third approach to standard setting: judgments based on analysis of group results. In this approach, students who took the test are separately rated as masters and nonmasters of the discipline. Masters are students who are deemed competent (because they have mastered the material) or who have exhibited the desired traits. Nonmasters are students who are not competent or do not possess the desired traits. The cutoff score should discriminate between these groups of masters and nonmasters. The chief advantage of this procedure is its reliance on how students perform rather than on what is represented on the test (Shepard, 1980). Zieky and Livingston (1977) and Huynh (1976) provide more in-depth discussions of how to determine a cutoff level using this contrasting-groups approach.

The three methods discussed often produce varying cutoff

levels. In addition, some arbitrariness remains in choice of procedure or choice of judges. <u>Which judgment does one accept, the average of the judges or the lowest level of any judge?</u> Glass (1978) and Shepard (1980) maintain that, because these standard-setting approaches are arbitrary, cutoff levels should be determined through a *relative* comparison with other students. That is, the cutoff should be set by selecting a percentile rank from norm-referenced tables. They argue that a standard cannot be evaluated until comparative norms are available.

So now the discussion has come full circle. Again, one problem with the norm-referenced approach is that it is essentially a ranking of individuals, and this ranking (for instance, the 60th percentile) may not reflect particular qualitative levels, such as whether the students who scored at that level are competent or know the material. A cutoff score based on a set percentile could be selected arbitrarily without considering the difficulty of an examination or the characteristics of the sample on which the norm group is based. The 40th percentile is quite different for norms based on graduate school–bound seniors (such as the Graduate Record Examination's subject examination) than it is for norms based on typical graduating seniors. Also, the same score may be deemed a failing score one year and a passing score the next year because the associated percentile ranks change based on the sample of the two norm groups. What the student knows may not change, but his or her position relative to other students in the norm group may change. This change in norms from year to year actually occurs now on some of the tests used in higher education assessment. No doubt, this debate about the setting of standards by absolute criteria or by relative means using percentiles in norm groups will continue.

Comparing Groups of Students

<u>Why do some students score or rate higher than</u> other students? Do some students gain more or less over time than other students of similar ability or at a similar stage of development? What educational experiences are working well? What aspects of the campus environment are associated with higher outcomes? In some sit-

uations, it may be possible to study differences among randomly assigned groups of students, with each group representing a different type of educational program. If one group of students scores higher than another, it might be presumed that one type of educational program is better. Invariably, some aspect of the campus environment, whether it is an academic course or a student affairs program, is more effective than other aspects. Just as likely, some types of programs work better than others for some kinds of students.

The purpose of any model for analyzing assessment information is to document the contribution, or lack of contribution, of a particular educational program. The term *educational program* here includes any aspect of the campus environment that might influence students' behavior. It could be an instructional program, such as a major, an honors track, an off-campus study program, or a liberal studies curriculum. It could also be a combination of particular courses within an instructional program. Are certain courses or patterns of courses associated with student learning? Is there a difference between students who completed the minimum program requirements and students who completed extra coursework beyond the requirements? Are educational experiences such as independent study, fieldwork, research, and practicums associated with higher outcome measures?

As Cross and Angelo (1988) point out, assessment should be more concerned with the effectiveness of educational programs or experiences than with the overall certification process of graduates. For the typical faculty or student affairs staff member, the major value of assessment is to improve existing programs. Consequently, the aim of most assessment programs should be to determine the unique effects or net effects of the educational experiences (Pascarella, 1987b). Stated another way, institutions may want to document the "causes" of any positive change in students' learning and development. What caused students to learn more? Unfortunately, several problems stand in the way of the kind of study necessary to draw any conclusions about causality. The drawing of cause-and-effect conclusions requires a "scientific" approach, in which persons are randomly selected and randomly assigned to *control* and *experimental* groups. From a broad perspective, the experimental group would be exposed to higher education, the control group would not attend college, and the groups would be compared on common outcome measures to show, it is expected, that the experimental group performed better on the average. Of course, individual students cannot be randomly assigned to college and noncollege groups. People and institutions participate in this selection process deliberately, so that differences emerge between attenders and non-attenders before any educational intervention takes place. Many of the background characteristics that are closely associated with end-of-college outcomes "are also major determinants of whether or not one attends college, the type of college attended, if one chooses to go, and the extent and quality of involvement in different academic and social experiences during college" (Pascarella, 1987b, p. 5). It becomes difficult, then, to separate what students bring with them from what they experience in college or demonstrate they can do or be at the end of college. For example, if a student does well on an achievement test in his or her major as a graduating senior, is it because the student had high scholastic ability as an entering freshman? If a student demonstrates a high degree of moral development at graduation, is it because that person had a high sense of ethics as a beginning freshman?

But even though the typical approach of designing an experiment with control and experimental groups is impractical or impossible, it is still informative to compare one group of students with another group. The ethics of such practices should always be considered, of course, and care should be taken before students are placed in a particular educational program. (The ethics of assessment will be discussed in the next chapter.)

Although experimental studies are rare in higher education assessment programs, one example will be discussed here for illustrative purposes. At one institution, a number of complaints were received about roommate assignments in the residence halls. Roommate changes were common, and a number of students had allegedly dropped out of school because of problems with living conditions. Furthermore, the residence hall administrators were interested in exploring ways of improving students' personal development through the residence hall experience.

An experimental study was designed in which freshmen were randomly assigned roommates according to three groups of roommate matches. Students were previously assessed for their level of maturity as revealed on Heath's (1977) Perceived Self Questionnaire (PSQ), which was administered during freshman orientation. On the basis of their PSQ score, entering freshmen were classified as either high or low in maturity and were randomly assigned roommates in three groups: two high-maturity students as roommates, two low-maturity students, and a high- and a low-maturity student. The purpose of the study was to determine whether a student's change in maturity was due to the influence of the roommate. Would two low-maturity roommates support each other and mature faster? Would a high-maturity student pull up or positively influence a low-maturity student? Which set of roommates would be more compatible? Students in this study were then reassessed with the PSQ one semester later, and the PSQ averages were compared among the three groups of roommate matches for possible differences (Erwin, 1983a). Such studies are infrequent, but if the opportunity is available and the study is ethically feasible, experimental studies can furnish powerful evidence of program value. In the roommate study, the two high-maturity and the two low-maturity roommates increased in one aspect of maturity, but the high-low roommates did not.

Because experimental studies in assessment are impractical, quasi-experimental studies (Campbell and Stanley, 1966; Campbell, 1969; Weiss, 1972), or modified alternatives to true experimental studies, must be used. These alternatives include (1) the before-and-after study, also called pretest-posttest; (2) the after-only study, or posttest only; (3) the nonequivalent control group study; (4) comparisons of alternative group options; (5) time-series designs; and (6) causal modeling. There are problems with each approach; however, the option of randomly assigning students to various life or institutional experiences and of studying "pure" effects is usually not open to us.

The first two analytical approaches—the *before-and-after* study of a single program and the *after-only* study of the program (Weiss, 1972)—try to compensate for the fact that groups are not selected randomly by controlling statistically for those background characteristics that might interfere with one's outcome measures. The analytical model is intended both to study program effects and to eliminate nonprogram effects that could be used to explain differences in learning among various groups of students. For example, students in study-abroad programs might have enrolled because of their prior travel experiences or other aspects of their background. Thus, the students who participate in study-abroad programs may tend to be the more affluent students. Would students from lower economic backgrounds gain as much from study-abroad experiences?

The before-and-after model is also commonly referred to as a pretest-posttest, valued-added, or talent development approach (Astin, 1982, 1988). In this model, the student at the beginning of the program is the "control group," and the same student at the completion of the program is the "experimental group." Differences or changes in the student at the end of the designated program or curriculum are noted. The greater the change, the greater the effect attributed to the institutional program.

Pretests are especially useful when some students enter the designated program with some amount of learning or development already accrued. For example, if a student is majoring in mathematics or English, he or she may enter the collegiate institution as a freshman already possessing some knowledge in the major. The assessment is aimed at measuring contributions made by the institution and controlling for the fact that some students enter at more or less advanced levels. On the other hand, some programs may correctly presume that student majors enter the program with little or no knowledge of the field. For example, students majoring in finance have usually had little exposure to this field in prior high school coursework. Every department can make its own case for the necessity of pretesting, based on the discipline, the area to be assessed, and the background of students entering the program. Older students, for example, may be more likely to matriculate with knowledge of finance from the working world than an eighteen-year-old freshman would have. The pretest is also of interest when student development areas are being assessed. Presumably, all students enter the institution at some level of cognitive, moral, and psychosocial development, though these levels vary.

At least three problems are inherent in the before-and-after model. First, when students are followed longitudinally, or over a period of time, some positive changes usually will occur as a result of the students' maturation, rather than any contribution of the institution. For example, suppose that an institution wants to determine whether students have developed autonomy or independence as a result of their educational experiences. Would the positive change between the scores of entering freshmen and graduating seniors on the Student Development Task and Lifestyle Inventory's (Winston and Miller, 1987) Autonomy subscale be attributed to institutional effects or to maturation effects?

A second problem occurs when students drop out of school or out of an educational program. Is the posttest average higher than the pretest average because students who were not learning or developing dropped out? Perhaps the absence of dropouts' scores in the posttest average makes the effects of the program appear greater than they actually are.

A third problem is an artifact of statistics. Change scores have their own reliability, just as pretest and posttest measures do. Any measurement errors in the pretest or posttest items are compounded in these change scores. Furthermore, the higher the relationship of the pretest measures to the posttest scores, the less reliable are the change scores. This problem is messy from a technical viewpoint. For example, a student who scores 98 out of a possible 100 points on the pretest will be less likely to demonstrate improvement in a program than a student with an initial score of 40. This "low ceiling" on the pretest translates into lack of precision of measurement or potentially misleading information from some value-added designs. Fortunately, as Feldt and Brennan (1989, p. 127) illustrate, this phenomenon applies primarily to individual scores and not necessarily to group averages. Nevertheless, even changes in group averages require special technical interpretations.

To help overcome these problems, certain statistical designs for analysis, called analysis of covariance and preplanned regression models, are helpful. (The discussion here is not meant to instruct the reader in the intricacies of statistical models, but to point out the advantages of selected techniques. Those not trained in statistics may wish to consult a statistician.) Analysis of covariance or a regression design allows one to even out the differences of students on background characteristics that may interfere with the primary outcomes of interest. For example, students matriculate at varying ages and levels of academic ability. By covarying on characteristics such as age for development (Pascarella, 1987b) or SAT scores for ability, these statistical designs allow one to study measures of development or learning as if everyone had the same age or equal SAT scores. These statistical designs are not as effective as the randomization process in a true experimental design, but they offer considerable advantage in analysis over error-fraught change or difference scores or ratings.

The after-only design is probably one of the most popular analytical models that educators can use; yet it is one of the weakest approaches mentioned in this chapter for program improvement. If the only information a department has is the information collected at the end of the program, very little can be attributed directly to the effectiveness of the program's components. At best, the information collected may have value in and of itself for descriptive purposes, but not for explanatory purposes (Cook and Shadish, 1986). For instance, if the department uses a competency or criterion-referenced approach, it is useful to know the number of students reaching mastery levels in the desired areas. Obviously, if an unexpected number of students do not demonstrate knowledge or competency for a particular assessed objective, preparation should be bolstered to help future students meet that objective. Of course, what aspect of the program should be bolstered cannot be determined unless further analyses are conducted.

A more useful approach enables the educator to compare different subgroups of students within a single program. This approach is called the *nonequivalent control group* design. In this approach, available students are used as a comparison group with the designated group of students under particular study. However, available students are not always comparable students. This control group is not randomly determined and may be different from students entering the program under study. The goal in choosing the "control group" is to select members who have as many as possible of the same characteristics as people who will actually participate in the program. For example, student activities departments often conduct semester-long programs in enhancing leadership. Students enrolled in the leadership workshops are the target group under study. A nonequivalent control group of students waiting to enroll in the workshop might be assessed at the beginning and end of the semester for comparison purposes.

If the designated group for study was selected for participation or the students selected themselves to participate, the educator must try to select the nonequivalent control group to match the characteristics of the selected group. Admittedly, one does not always know the characteristics that led students to choose to participate in a given program, but the assessment study must try to approximate the groups as logically and conveniently as possible. The goal of such a design is, of course, the equivalency of the groups at the beginning of the program (Campbell, 1969; Weiss, 1972).

In addition to the common approach of comparing students in a designated educational program with students in some type of control group, it is desirable to compare subgroups of students in *alternative program options* (Oetting and Cole, 1978). An institution may compare the average outcome scores of students who took language literature courses, those who took English literature courses, and those who took philosophy courses to fulfill a general education or liberal arts distribution requirement. Which group of courses resulted in greater learning? In student affairs, how should financial aid money be allocated? Should it be awarded as scholarships, as loans, or as work-study? If work-study students had higher autonomy scores or better-developed career plans than students receiving only loans or scholarships, there might be policy implications for allocating monies among these financial aid alternatives (Erwin and Love, 1989). Is a cooperative experience better than an off-campus internship experience or an on-campus practicum? It may be meaningful to construct or conceptualize alternative educational experiences for analyzing differences in outcome measures.

In addition to quasi-experimental studies, time-series and causal models are other analytical models for consideration. In *time-series* designs, measurements for a given assessment method are plotted over time. For instance, an academic department may make annual assessments with the same instrument over a period of several years. Time-series methods enable one to discover earlier patterns to explain short-term fluctuations. Dramatic rises or falls from one year to the next year may be indicative of recurrent or larger trends that cannot be detected when only two points in time are compared (Linn and Slinde, 1977; Weiss, 1972).

A more complex statistical type of analytical design, called *causal modeling,* adds sophistication to studies of college impact (Pascarella, 1987b). It will be mentioned only briefly because it is too technical for a full and adequate discussion here. Causal modeling attempts to go beyond simply describing relationships between outcome measures and collegiate environmental influences and beyond predicting how well students will perform. Causal modeling is an "integrated system of hypotheses to explain" various causal relationships among measures of student collegiate involvement and stated outcome measures (Miller and Wilson, 1983, p. 14). In a typical causal model, one usually includes the various input measures of the matriculating student, such as scholastic ability, personal characteristics, or pretest values of learning and development; the multiple measures of various influences of the campus environment, such as courses taken or student affairs programs participated in; and various outcome measures. The measures in the model are related in a longitudinal scheme and studied for cause-and-effect relationships.

Content Analysis

Many assessment programs begin with a review of existing portfolios, written records, or an interview and survey of students. The initial interviews and surveys usually are loosely structured, and open-ended responses are sought instead of answers to very specific questions or prompts. From these interviews and surveys come more specifically designed rating scales and structured questionnaires. One of the early problems in collecting open-ended responses is how to analyze the information in some meaningful form. Content analysis offers one method for summarizing the information gleaned from unstructured transcripts or written reports.

Content analysis is a systematic process for categorizing the content of written and, occasionally, oral communications. It is usually applied in assessment work to the study of responses to open-ended questions on a survey. However, free forms of responses might also be available from portfolios, diaries, supervisors' ratings, or other archival records. Content analysis is different from ethnographic observational methods because the data for analysis are usually written responses or oral communications (Riley and Stoll, 1968).

Faculty and student affairs staff often use open-ended questions on alumni surveys. In these and other surveys or narrative materials, the respondent produces an unrestricted written response. Because no restrictions are placed on the answer, the respondent often provides information that might not have been anticipated beforehand, or that would not have been suggested to the person through a forced-choice technique such as multiple-choice options. Open-ended questions are particularly useful in the beginning stages of survey building or for probing students' experiences. Although most educators might predict or have expectations about typical students' responses, the content categories derived from open-ended questions invariably offer alternatives to consider. Often, selective-response survey statements can be written on the basis of the first group's open-ended responses and then administered to the next group of persons.

After the open-ended responses obtained from surveys or narrative materials are read, content analysis, in its simplest form, requires the formulation of a small number of categories from the recurring themes or patterns that appear in the open-ended responses. What are the repeatable words, phrases, or sentences that summarize an idea, concept, or feeling and are mentioned throughout the narrative feedback? For example, alumni's responses to the survey question "What suggestions would you offer to improve the education you received at ABC institution?" might yield the following categories: "additional computer training or coursework," "training in writing," "support services for career placement," and so on. Analysis of these categories can include what was stated, how it was stated, or how often it was stated. Or, for more in-depth analysis, the characteristics of these alumni can be explained according to the substance, or category, of content. For instance, do the alumni who wanted more computer training have any common characteristics? Were they in particular majors? What courses in computing did they have, if any, and how well did they do as undergraduates?

Content analyses of group interviews with students who scored or rated particularly high or low on assessment instruments could prove useful. Sometimes it is not known why some students do particularly well or particularly poorly. These students' performances often contradict other evidence, such as grade point average or the faculty's perceptions. Content analyses of these interviews can offer insight into possible program weaknesses, insights that can be confirmed or disconfirmed by further study. For example, an institution administered the Erwin Identity Scale (Erwin and Delworth, 1980, 1982) to measure its entering freshman class's identity levels. New freshmen who scored below the 10th percentile were interviewed individually to determine how they could be helped. The interviews confirmed the hypothesis that these students were considering dropping out of school. In addition, it was discovered through content analysis that these low-identity freshmen were having difficulties in adjusting to college because they were homesick. A special student affairs program was designed to help these students adjust to moving away from home and living on their own.

More complex strategies for coding unrestricted responses are discussed by Riley and Stoll (1968).

Interpreting Assessment Information

Interpreting assessment information is more than describing or generalizing about the assessment information in a statistical sense. It is explaining what the data mean in practical terms. Although a statistician or person trained in assessment may assist in the data analyses, the persons associated with the educational programs under study must be involved in interpreting the analyses, just as they should have been involved from the beginning in determining the program objectives and questions of interest. The program-centered approach to interpretation is an extension of the "stakeholders" philosophy of evaluation; that is, people who are fully involved in the entire evaluation process, particularly in ascribing meaning and value to the data, are more likely to implement the results of an evaluation (Guba and Lincoln, 1981). Although a superb assessment study may have been planned, its success and subsequent interpretation will hinge on its being carried out effectively and according to plan.

After the intervention program, educational program experience, or aspect of the campus environment has been selected for study, the monitoring questions suggested by Oetting and Cole (1978, pp. 44–46) can help ensure that the assessment study does not drift from what was intended.

1. "Is the educational program doing what was planned?" Sometimes a program's objectives change in the middle of the study, and one's initially planned outcome measures no longer match the program objectives. Therefore, one should plan for program adjustments, such as adopting new outcome measures. Assessment is dynamic, not static.

2. "Is the educational program under study achieving its objectives effectively?" Suppose that computer training is required of honors sophomores, so that they can conduct their thesis research more efficiently. If the students fail to implement their computer training and continue to do hand analyses, they may not maintain their proficiency in computing into the senior year, although the training program might have been effective at the time of training.

3. "Are program parts equally effective?" Some staff members may lack commitment to assessment, and this lack of commitment may translate into lackadaisical participation in some alternative educational programs. In such instances, any lack of effectiveness of these alternative strategies may be confused with poor staff implementation.

4. "Does the educational program maintain its effectiveness?" Occasionally, excitement in the initial stages of a program wanes in its later stages. In addition, the effective educational program may lose its impact after the assessment study is completed.

5. "Are students responding as planned?" Varying motivational levels and unplanned competing interests often interfere with the best-intended program structure. This issue was discussed

in Chapter Two, with reference to strategies for collecting assessment information.

6. "Are some students reached more effectively than others?" If the educational program is not delivered equally to all students, generalizations about its effectiveness are weakened. Is the major targeted only for graduate school–bound students? Do students housed in particular residential halls receive preferential treatment?

7. "Is the program meeting goals other than those expected?" For example, the aim of many freshman orientation programs is to help students plan short-term educational goals and make the transition from home to college. Questionnaires could be selected or designed to measure students' progress toward career decisiveness and autonomy. On the other hand, the orientation program may also serve other needs, such as public relations for parents, which might not be obvious.

8. "Is the assessment plan being followed?" Sometimes, to prevent further delays in meeting requests for a program, staff will reach out to students on waiting lists. The waiting list was, of course, serving as a control group for comparison purposes. Changing this control group threatens any conclusions that might be drawn about differences between the program group and the control group.

9. "Is anything happening that might distort the data?" In one state, officials announced that teacher undergraduate education majors would be abolished. The resulting loss of morale among students and faculty interfered with assessment studies currently under way.

10. "What are the real costs of the educational program?" Assessment personnel usually do not compile or evaluate the economic costs of an educational program; however, future uses of assessment results may dictate examination of costs. Cost of space, time, and personnel might be reported for the current program and alternative program options.

Brinkerhoff, Brethower, Hluchkyj, and Nowakowski (1983) also offer several guidelines for interpreting assessment information. In particular, they suggest that educators "formulate and explain interpretations in light of contextual and confirming, limiting, or disconfirming information; cite limitations and clearly explain degrees of certainty warranted; provide alternative explanations and interpretations where appropriate; [and] seek out and include 'minority' opinions on opposing interpretations when appropriate" (p. 147).

In addition, educators should avoid presenting a totally rosy picture, stating that no problems exist in an institution's programs. Most reviewers at the state or agency level are alerted by interpretations reporting only glowing findings and excellent progress of students. Problems always exist in programs, and that should be reported. Limitations of the sample, the methods, and the analytical model used should also be reported. If possible, educators should explain why students are performing at lower-than-expected competency levels, or why students in one group outperform students in other groups. If they do not know why, they should at least offer hypotheses for further study.

Conclusion

Analyzing assessment information can be a complex task, just as interpreting the findings is a particularly responsible task. Sometimes these steps are viewed as the whole of assessment; however, they build upon prior planning processes. As with other steps, these steps probably require the ideas of several people. The issue of what is done with the results and findings is discussed in the next chapter.

EIGHT

Reporting and Using Assessment Information

This chapter discusses several strategies for reporting the results and conclusions derived from interpretations of assessment information. Careful reporting is essential if educators hope to avoid a problem that experienced evaluators complain of—namely, that decision makers seldom act on the empirical information given them (Brown, Braskamp, and Newman, 1978; Weiss, 1972). Another problem concerning the use of assessment information has been pointed out by Cook and Shadish (1986), who claim that "evaluation is in many ways just another political act that occurs in a context where power, ideology, and interest are more powerful determinants of decision making than feedback about program" (p. 200). How can educators adopt reporting strategies that will allow assessment information to contribute in positive ways to the decision-making process in higher education? How can the communication process be established to meet the needs of those who request or who might use the information? Fortunately, some helpful guidelines for reporting strategies are available from communications and evaluation professionals. As in other chapters, these strategies do not stand alone, but build on the prior assessment steps of establishing clear purposes, objectives, and analytical methods.

132

Factors Influencing the Use of Results

According to Brown, Braskamp, and Newman (1978); Thompson, Brown, and Furgason (1981); and Whitman and Foster (1987), three major factors influence the use of results for decision making: the source of the information, the channel or mode for the information, and the audience for the information. Other sources (Fishbein and Ajzen, 1975; Newman, Brown, and Littman, 1979) describe this process as *who* says *what* to *whom*. In the discussion below, the process becomes *"who* says *what* and *how* to *whom"*—so that four factors, rather than three, are delineated: the source, the mode of presentation, the message communicated, and the audience.

Although the settings described are not in higher education assessment work, some research does exist that demonstrates different ways audiences react to information. Important factors include the title of the evaluator (Braskamp, Brown, and Newman, 1978; Newman, Brown, and Littman, 1979), the language and style of the report (Brown, Braskamp, and Newman, 1978), the type of information provided (Brown, Newman, and Rivers, 1985), the professional experience of the audience (Newman, Brown, and Littman, 1979), and the perceived need of the audience for information (Brown, Braskamp, and Newman, 1978; Bull and Newman, 1986).

The Source of the Information. The source of assessment results is a person or group functioning as communicator, compiler, and overall coordinator of the assessment process. Essentially, it is the person or group of people who conducted and wrote the assessment study. Generally, one of three types of people or groups will serve as the responsible source for the assessment report: the respective faculty or student affairs personnel (the intrainstitutional group); an assessment specialist, institutional researcher, or administrator (the interinstitutional group); and the state or accreditation agency personnel (the external group). In some instances, particularly if a state mandate exists, it is common for all three sources to be involved.

According to Brown (1978), the source must be credible in order for the results to be accepted. Credibility is determined by one's expertise, program knowledge, objectivity, and ability to work with other people. Expertise comes from a knowledge of measurement and evaluation practices. Program knowledge comes from being a part of or studying closely the specific program. Objectivity includes fairness both to the needs of the service providers and to the audience requesting the assessment.

Assessment results are best used for program improvement when the source and the audience are the same. Therefore, to encourage the use of the results for program improvement purposes, the respective faculty or student affairs personnel should compose the assessment report. This procedure—whereby the people who provide the services being evaluated are also the people who interpret and report the assessment information—is a departure from the structure of many evaluation studies of government-funded programs. In these evaluation efforts, an external source is typically called in to conduct and produce the study. Higher education, however, is different in its structure of governance from other organizations, and responsibilities for conducting and reporting assessment information will commonly reside in the individual academic or student affairs unit. This is particularly true for intradepartmental assessment in the major and for student development programs. If faculty or student affairs staff are responsible for the entire study, the results have more intrinsic value and are more likely to be used.

Interinstitutional efforts can reflect a different source, such as an assessment person, an institutional researcher, an administrator, a chairperson of a campus-wide committee effort, or a staff member in another department. For example, an administrator who is charged with overall campus assessment responsibilities might oversee general education or liberal studies assessment, because general education programs transcend several departments. Faculty and student development staff may carry heavy responsibilities in a liberal studies assessment project, but an overall coordinator is often viewed as the source. Other interinstitutional areas for assessment might be alumni follow-up surveys, basic skills testing, or objectives-across-the-curriculum assessment. Because the source of these assessments may lie outside any one department, the process and findings may be perceived as less credible by individual departments.

A last source of assessment information may be completely outside the institution. Examples of such sources are accreditation teams who collect and conduct evaluation studies or state officials who analyze data from basic skills tests. Credibility of the resulting reports is high for the external agency but probably lower in the institutional department, which may have had little input in the process. The key, of course, is for external sources to solicit input from within institutions. Texas, for example, established statewide assessment committees or sought ideas from all institutions possibly affected by any results.

Some research studies in evaluation have found that the title (Braskamp, Brown, and Newman, 1978) and gender (Newman, Brown, and Littman, 1979) of the source were associated with greater acceptance of the report (Braskamp, Brown, and Newman, 1978); however, much is still unknown about the role of the source in higher education assessment settings.

The Mode of Presentation. The way the message is delivered can also influence whether its recommendations are accepted or used. The mode or channel of delivery can take a variety of forms. Passon (1987) lists five types of reports that can be prepared: the progress report, the final report, the technical report, the summary, and the media presentation.

The *progress report* is one of a series of interim reports informing colleagues, administrators, and perhaps state officials how assessment projects are progressing. In a sense, assessment projects are always in progress, and every annual report is an interim report. Rarely does an assessment study about an ongoing program end in the short term. Results prompt further questions. Individual components of a program may not need to be examined oftener than every few years; however, few program review efforts end after a short one- or two-year study. Many assessment methods usually take several years to design, including pilot testing and redesign efforts. Furthermore, many problems graduate only a few students yearly, and it may take several years of data collection before any generalizations can be reasonably drawn. In these cases, an interim report may represent findings over a designated period of time. Programs and personnel change, and assessment reports become outdated; consequently, periodic progress reports are natural. Although some educators do not wish to view assessment as a long-term venture, it is reasonable to expect ongoing assessment reports because of the complexity of what is being measured. For instance, accreditation agencies have shifted their emphasis on self-study from a once-in-seven-years activity to a continuous systematic procedure.

Whatever the reason or requirement, it is useful to produce periodic progress reports or to view each annual report as a progress report about assessment activities. Audiences are more likely to tolerate delays and to accept findings if they are kept aware of progress. Reporting is not a one-way process but a two-way effort, with reactions to any assessment program's progress flowing from the audience back to the source of the assessment. This is another chance for the audience to have input into the process and for the purposes of the assessment to be supported.

For beginning assessment programs, these progress reports might be submitted more frequently, perhaps several times within the first year. The progress report can also be useful to spell out obstacles and limitations that might follow in the final report. Although preliminary findings may be included, this is mainly a time to tell about the progress of the study and provide a preview of upcoming activities (Passon, 1987). Especially under state mandates, institutions should seek numerous opportunities to share program start-up efforts in order to obtain state officials' reactions to directions and procedures. Institutions sharing frequent progress reports with state audiences may find themselves influencing state policy more than state policy influences their assessment activities.

Another major type of report frequently mentioned in evaluation literature is the *final report*. If assessment is considered a long-term or a permanent fixture, the term *final report* is a misnomer. Nevertheless, a final report may be issued as an annual, a biannual, or a ten-year report. Passon (1987) suggests that every "final report" should contain results, conclusions, judgments about the program, and recommendations for future action (p. 121). Passon also reminds us that the final report is a political as well as an informational document. Faculty and administrators are only too well aware of this, especially when the report is written for an audience outside the department under study.

Instead of providing balanced judgments about a program, some faculty sources may sanitize the final report, leaving out any negative findings. But glowing reports that "everything is great" can easily become lightning rods attracting further scrutiny or accusations of low standards. What was seen as an opportunity for bragging becomes an occasion for defending lack of rigor. All programs have problems, and it is naive to imply otherwise. Negative findings should be reported.

Individual institutions or agencies may have their own report format, but a typical assessment report may include the following sections: (1) Objectives: What is being assessed? (2) Methods: How are the objectives being assessed? (3) Results and Conclusions: What do the data say and what are the recommendations? (4) Uses: How were the data used? (5) Future: What questions remain and what new issues need to be addressed in future studies? The following outline shows the criteria, within these five report divisions, that are used at James Madison University.

I.   Comprehensiveness and Specificity of the Department's Objectives
   • Are the objectives stated as specific measurable outcomes rather than vague, global goals?
   • Do the objectives appear to cover the wide range of content topics expected in the discipline?
   • Do the objectives include goals for writing? Critical thinking? Library skills? Developmental objectives? Computing?
   • Was there peer review of the objectives?

II. Assessment Methods
   • How appropriate are the assessment methods for evaluating each departmental objective?
   • Was an externally created instrument considered?
   • Was an in-house instrument considered?
   • If an in-house instrument was adopted, how were the test items constructed?

- Is there evidence of reliability?
- Is there evidence of content validity (for example, table of specifications) in the assessment instrument?
- Are there other evidences of validity?
- Was there peer review of the assessment methods and instruments?
- Were the assessment procedures and sample described?

III. Analyses of Results
- Was the information summarized in a quantifiable form?
- Were narrative explanations of the meaning of the information provided?
- Is there a discussion of how well the assessment information meets the stated objectives?
- Has the department identified program strengths and weaknesses?
- Were outcome measures compared for alternative aspects of the program? Why are some people scoring higher or lower?

IV. Uses
- Has the department specified how the information obtained from assessment will be or was used?
- What program changes have been or will be made?
- What other recommendations based on the assessment information have been given?

V. Future Assessment Plans and Goals
- What questions will be addressed in future studies?
- What objectives will be covered in future reports that were not covered in this report?

Other evaluation researchers (Brown, 1978; Passon, 1987; Wolf, 1987) suggest a separate *technical* report, containing methodological and statistical analyses. These writers believe that final reports should not include heavy quantitative sections, because the technical parts distract the readers. For instance, the typical administrator does not have the background, desire, or time to wade through pages of technical data. Some audiences, however, are interested in the technical background of the methods and design, and it is for this group that a separate technical report might be written. If a separate technical report is not prepared, one might also consider including any methodological steps as an appendix to the final report. If any report is intended only for an intradepartmental focus, even less technical information may be necessary. If reports go off-campus, it is probably wise to include a technical section, an appendix, or a separate technical report, particularly if the external audience requests information about the quality of the methods used.

The *summary report* is the type of report preferred by most audiences of administrators and external constituents. Depending on the scope of the assessment program's activities, summary reports usually run up to thirteen pages in length. Osborne (1986) found that a thirteen-page summary was better received than a five-page summary in a simulation study with teachers. The focus of the summary is on the major findings and the action steps taken on the basis of the findings. Little is included about methodology or analytical design. Considering Ewell, Finney, and Lenth's (1990) perspective that most of our constituencies want assessment for program improvement, most summaries should reveal how the data are being used. Obviously, some overall statements will be made about the programs involved and the variety of assessment methods employed, but it is the use of the data that is of interest to most audiences. Summaries highlighting uses are powerful reports for any audience, inside or outside the institution.

The last type of report that Passon (1987) mentions is the *media report,* a frequent occurrence around the country. In some areas, assessment is a very visible activity, and it is best to prepare for the possibility of press coverage. If a centralized statewide testing program exists, published accounts of institutional averages are outside an institution's control. More typically, though, special media-directed reports might be considered to accompany a more comprehensive final report. Often, specially prepared media summaries can make positive results enhance an institution's image and can turn negative results targeted for improvement into positive gains. Media reports are often prepared in consultation with the institution's public affairs official.

Besides its presentation in written form, the report can also be communicated orally to enhance acceptance of the findings. Oral communication about all assessment activities with all involved parties is vital. Of course, different reports meet different audience needs. Moreover, the reporting process should be viewed not as a single act, such as a final report, but as a process. The reporting process is one of continuous and varying communication between source and audience. In a study of the differences between evaluation projects that were successfully implemented and those that were not, Glaser and Taylor (1973) found that the directors of successful evaluation projects held open discussions at the beginning and throughout the process.

Another form of reporting is the *case study*. The case-study approach to reporting is not a new method, but it remains powerfully descriptive (Schermerhorn and Williams, 1979). Instead of relying on numbers to portray the characteristics and patterns of students' learning and development, the case study describes a fictitious student, who represents the typical or average student from the analyses. Marcia Mentkowski of Alverno College was an early pioneer of reporting by constructing "conversations" from the typical student as they changed through the college process. Sarah Dingham's "letter to a friend" technique at the University of Arizona is another example of a typical student-reporting mechanism for individual feedback.

Instead of using only numbers in a table, report writers might also consider supplying graphs to chart the meaning of the information. A picture still conveys meaning to a broader audience than numbers, which can be threatening to some people. Advances in microcomputing now permit colorful charts and plots to be drawn by nontechnically oriented persons. Software such as Chart (Microsoft Corporation, 1985) or Harvard Graphics (Software Publishing Corporation, 1988) can be used to display trends over time or to draw comparisons among subgroups of students.

The Message Communicated. The findings included in the report can be positive, negative, or, more commonly, mixed. If the findings are positive, they will be well received by all audiences, and the assessment program will be well supported by administrators. If the findings are negative, or are perceived as negative, reactions can be swift and stunning, especially when the findings run counter to expectations. In many cases, negative findings are not new to faculty or student affairs educators, who may have been aware of the problems beforehand. If problems are discovered in unexpected areas, however, the people involved in these areas may become defensive and refuse to accept the findings. This defensiveness can occur at the departmental level and at upper levels of administration. Carter (1971) has outlined several reasons why people choose not to accept negative findings: (1) psychological characteristics of the persons responsible for the program; (2) the quality of the study; (3) the feasibility of implementing the findings; (4) past negative experiences with evaluation; and (5) inappropriateness of data or source to generate recommendations (p. 118).

If the decision makers for the program about which negative findings are generated are closely associated with the program, they are likely to perceive the negative findings as a threat. For example, if a program in the career development center has proved to be ineffective, the center's director may be the most threatened, especially if that director has initiated the program or has developed an emotional attachment to it. If a general studies program exhibits negative or no effects, the dean or vice president who oversees this program may be defensive about the findings. In addition, faculty may perceive negative findings as a threat to their worth and livelihood. Administrators may perceive negative findings as an affront to their competence and perhaps to their future in this and other administrative positions. Others may regard the findings as a threat to the institution, to which they have a strong loyalty. But regardless of these possible threats to self-concepts, the closer the audience is to the program, the more the need for the information exists (Carter, 1971; Brown, 1978; Bull and Newman, 1986).

When the data suggest problems of quality throughout the institution, the conclusions of the assessment report are especially likely to be challenged as erroneous. First, the assessment methods will be challenged. Are the methods really appropriate for the program that was studied? Are the methods accurate? If the methods were poorly designed or chosen without regard to the program objectives, these weaknesses will be used to discredit the findings. Unfortunately, such weaknesses have been found at many institutions that chose the ACT's College Outcome Measures Project and ETS's Academic Profile as assessment methods without regard to their validity for the institutions' basic studies programs. Results were often low because the instrument did not measure what the institution was trying to teach. Not only was the instrument rejected, but the assessment program in general was then called into question by the findings. Second, if the assessment methods hold up to scrutiny in the face of negative results, the sample and the analytical design are questioned. Did enough students participate? Did the students take the assessment seriously? Were appropriate analytical methods used? If any flaws in the sample or design are discovered, the negative findings are usually dismissed as meaningless. Third, the source of the assessment study will be challenged. Did the person or persons who conducted the study involve all necessary parties? Was this person sensitive to the process and people involved? Is the source qualified and competent to draw these interpretations and conclusions? Occasionally, colleagues and administrators may complain that the person conducting the study and disclosing institutional weaknesses is being disloyal to the institution.

Sometimes the findings suggest that additional resources, or shifts in services or personnel, are necessary. These findings may be rejected on the grounds that the changes are not feasible. For instance, many institutions, particularly in the private sector, may not have the necessary resources or services or personnel for bolstering weak areas.

Finally, decision makers may reject negative findings because they have had unfortunate past experiences with testing or evaluation. These past experiences can block not only the assessment process but also any use of assessment results, no matter how sound or beneficial the recommendations are. Some educators outright reject the use of assessment methods based on human performance for program review, claiming that educational impact can never be measured.

What, then, should be done to ensure that negative findings

will be accepted? First of all, the person or persons conducting the assessment study should reexamine what led to the conclusions, even though the study may not be completed. After confirming that the prior assessment steps of method design or selection are sound, the person conducting the study should inform the ranking unit administrator about the negative findings. This administrator may be a department head, a dean, or a vice president. Faculty and staff also should be informed about the preliminary findings, even though a final report has not been written. In the event of preliminary negative results, it is also beneficial to consider alternative explanations for the results. For example, when a new part of the program has been found ineffective, is it perhaps because students of lower ability or development have been in the program from the beginning? In order to answer such questions, one should select the most powerful analytical design available, thereby eliminating any extraneous variables that might explain program impact or lack of impact. Because negative results have such powerful effects on service providers and administrators, foreseeing alternative interpretations of the data increases the acceptance of any findings.

In addition to these more technical matters, the communication skills of the campus assessment coordinators are critical at this time. If open communication was already established between source and audience, the acceptability of negative findings should be increased. Sensitivity to the individuals involved in the program under question must be shown. Moreover, the findings should be reported in a positive manner, with an emphasis on the improvements that can result from the assessment. As Donald Lumsden of Kean College points out, when assessment is undertaken for improvement purposes, there are no "negative" findings. And as Wergin (1989) reminds us, it is the positive results and side effects of assessment that must receive the most attention. The process of having educators talk with one another is itself a positive outcome of assessment. It is this focus on constructive events that will move assessment forward.

The fear associated with negative findings occasionally prevents educators from conducting future forthright assessment efforts. In actuality, programs are rarely discontinued just because an assessment or evaluation study has found them ineffective (Cook and Shadish, 1986). The need for the program led to its creation, and that need probably still exists. Commonly, any results about program ineffectiveness only suggest that improvements in the program are necessary.

The timing of the assessment report can also affect the way in which the results are perceived. If the planning or analysis phases are prolonged, interest in the findings can wane or be lost. Similarly, assessment studies are more likely to be used at the initiation of a new program. A program or service that has been in place for years is harder to change. Timing of the message also means that the message may have to be repeated several times to get the main point across to an institutional audience (Halput, 1966). Possibly the same findings can be communicated through different types of reports or different media, or the same assessment study might be replicated with a different group of students or with a different assessment method. The larger the potential impact of the findings, the greater the need for accumulated assessment evidence to substantiate and reinforce the point.

Either descriptive or explanatory content messages may also be conveyed in a report. A descriptive report reduces a large volume of data to simple, digestible statements about levels of learning or development. It usually reports the percent of students scoring above the competency level or the simple average on a given outcome. An explanatory report, instead of simply describing characteristics of the student group, explains why these students are learning or developing at their given levels. Whereas the descriptive report merely outlines how well the students performed, the explanatory report indicates why some students performed better than other students. The descriptive report may meet the requirements of an external agency for accountability; however, only the explanatory type of report suggests what works well and what does not. The explanatory report studies various aspects of the campus environment and the influence they have on levels of learning and development. The information gained from the explanatory study suggests avenues for working changes into the program. It suggests what programs work well and what aspects of the program are not associated with higher scores or score gains.

Anderson and Ball (1978) claim that the main shortcoming

of many reports is the absence of steps for action. A descriptive
report usually does not address program options, as does the
explanatory report. For some aspects, it is not clear to the decision
maker what should or should not be done. The right questions
might have been addressed and a technically sound study produced;
however, unclear or ambiguous conclusions can leave the reader
with no direction for change. Anderson and Ball also point out that
the results can be too fragile to make points convincingly. Myers
(1970) reminded evaluators years ago that data should support decisions to be made, not decisions that have already been made.

The Audience for the Information. The audience for the as-   4
sessment report is as important as its source or its mode of presentation or its message. Since the report is produced for an audience,
it should address itself to that audience's needs. Morris, Fitz-
Gibbon, and Freeman (1987) remind us that "some users do not
know what they need." Furthermore, "different users want different
information—even to answer the same questions;" and "for some
users, the information needs change during the course of the evaluation" (pp. 14–15). These issues are particularly relevant for the
assessment movement because state mandates are still evolving, because different audiences need different information for different
purposes, and because program objectives and assessment methods
frequently change at the beginning of assessment efforts. In addition to being relevant, assessment findings must be practical, useful,
credible, understandable, and timely (Morris, Fitz-Gibbon, and
Freeman, 1987, pp. 20–21).

Regardless of how the source perceives the importance of the
message, the audience must perceive its value before any action is
taken. As Bull and Newman (1986) and Windle and Ochberg (1975)
have pointed out, different audiences use the same information in
different ways. Four major groups will read or hear assessment reports: the faculty or student affairs staff that deliver the program
services; institutional committees, such as a curriculum committee;
the institution's administrators, such as a dean, vice president, or
president; and the external staff, such as state officials or accreditation review teams.

In the past, the audience consisted primarily of the faculty or student affairs staff within the respective department and also, to some extent, the upper-level administrators at an institution. Self-study reports were submitted only infrequently to outside review teams. External demands for assessment have changed these habits. More people or audiences outside the institution are interested in the quality of what goes on inside the institution, and audiences inside and outside the institution are viewing these reports more critically because of the assessment charges. Therefore, although assessment may be conducted at an institution primarily for its own improvement, institutions should consider producing a report periodically for external audiences as well.

Recommendations for Action

As was previously discussed, two types of reports can be produced: the descriptive or narrative report and the explanatory or persuasive report (House, 1977), including alternatives for action (Cook, Leviton, and Shadish, 1985). The descriptive report outlines basic assessment activities at the institution: "What are the program's effects?" "How many students achieved the intended objectives?" The explanatory report outlines steps for action based on the assessment results: "Why did one group of students perform better or worse than another group?" "What are the effects of the various program alternatives?" In a broad sense, programs may be supported, modified, or eliminated. Will the institution's administration support departmental needs for additional resources? Will pilot results indicating effectiveness prompt the adoption of a program at the institution? Will the inadequacies in a program be recognized and addressed?

Probably most assessment reports in final form will suggest several alternatives for action. The source conducting the study naturally hopes that these recommendations will be adopted. If the source and the audience are the same, the chances for adoption are, of course, greater. If the audience is different from the source, the message becomes a persuasive document for the audience. If assessment is integral to the functions of the institution, it is natural to expect that assessment results will enter into the resource allocation process. For instance, if a deficiency is documented from assessment results, a dean or vice president may allocate resources to improve a program's weakness. The same concept applies at the state level for public institutions. If an institution discovers and documents a weakness to the state, an accompanying petition might be submitted requesting funds to bolster the deficiency. In general, states are more receptive to this data-based approach than to automatically requested budget increases annually.

Past evaluation theorists (for example, Weiss, 1972) have lamented the volume of studies that contain no recommendations for action. Of course, some faculty and administrators desire no action by outside parties and are happy to go through assessment exercises for no other purpose than mere compliance. On the other end of the continuum, for those who wish to improve their programs, how can useful assessment results be implemented?

In reality, decisions are not based exclusively on information available in the organization. Decisions are based partly on political considerations regardless of what the data show (Wergin, 1976, 1989; Brown, 1978; Weiss, 1981). Administrators may act on friendship, immediate tensions, current moods, subjects' conversations, costs, or deference to preserve an image or reputation (Brown, 1978). For example, how many institutions have chosen not to use norm-referenced instruments because of possible comparisons with other institutions?

In addition, actions, however soundly based, are not always immediately forthcoming. Some decision makers wait for the *perfect* data (Ewell, 1988a) and the *perfect* assessment study before acting. Or information from an assessment report may go into an administrator's mental file, where it competes against other influences, including costs for changes; lack of staff expertise in deficient areas; students' resistance; and other institutional priorities, such as community service. Sometimes decisions are delayed even if the assessment information is ultimately used. That is, the conclusions may be adopted only after considerable time has elapsed between the report and the eventual action (Weiss, 1981). Wergin (1976) and others have suggested that new models for decision making must be created to ensure that information will be used promptly and appropriately and not simply to legitimate decisions that have already been made (Brown, 1978; Weiss, 1981).

Admittedly, some studies are too stilted, with strict use of random assignments and controlled conditions, and therefore produce findings that are too narrow for any benefit. In this case, practice is not served, and the assessment process does not support the inherent questions initially of interest about a program's effectiveness. Sometimes, however, excessively dramatic conclusions are expected from assessment, and the lack of clear results can disappoint the eager, primed audience. In such instances, educators should assist decision makers by suggesting how the information might be used.

Cook and Shadish (1986) and Weiss (1977) propose their concept of "enlightenment," in which information is available on an ongoing basis. The past model of submitting action alternatives in a dramatic movement for action through a formal report is not always realistic. Instead, information should be disseminated informally as well as formally to several audiences, to support the long-run functioning of the institution. The enlightenment approach encourages clarification of program objectives, needs, and relationships among faculty, staff, administrators, and external agency officials. At the least, open and continuous communication calls for valued relationships in which information is collected and exchanged to meet multiple needs.

Unfortunately, the enlightenment approach may not be sufficient to satisfy the new audiences of state legislators, governors, parents, and the public. If current pressures from these audiences remain, assessment reports may have to appeal to external standards, not just internal standards, for higher education. It is unclear what these external expectations will be, but relevance to the workplace and society will probably receive priority. It is possible that media reports about assessment information will become more common, to appeal to concerned taxpayers and prospective students. Assessment reports will be written, no doubt, for others as well as for ourselves.

Ethics of Assessment

In reporting assessment information, institutions must always observe ethical standards, such as those contained in the *Standards for*

Evaluation of Educational Programs, Projects, and Materials, as outlined by a Joint Committee on Standards for Educational Evaluation (1981), representing twelve evaluation organizations. It covers four areas of evaluation: utility, feasibility, propriety, and accuracy. Another useful source is a statement of standards for test developers and users by a joint committee representing the American Psychological Association, the American Educational Research Association, and the National Council on Measurement in Education (Committee to Develop Standards for Educational and Psychological Testing, 1985). Anderson and Ball (1978), Guba (1975), and Riecken and Boruch (1974) have also written about potential ethical problems in evaluation. As these writers indicate, three major elements of ethics are particularly important in higher education assessment: accuracy, quality, and confidentiality.

Departments and institutions have an obligation to report *accurately* the results of assessment (Guba, 1975). In reports to an institution's audiences, both the strengths and the weaknesses of the program under review should be noted. As Wolf (1987) points out, it is often tempting to suppress "unflattering results." Departments are often reluctant to admit problems to upper-level administrators, and administrators are often reticent about releasing negative findings outside their institutions. The media report can help perform this task successfully. In addition, it is often helpful to describe the action that has been taken to rectify a weakness, since external audiences tend to view efforts for improvement or for "moving forward" in a positive light. Accuracy also dictates that evaluation results should not be made to appear more negative than the data support (Guba, 1975). On rare occasions, institutions have reported such results in order to gain extra funding or to elicit support from the outside to effect a major institutional change. Clearly, such reporting is unethical.

Departments and institutions also have an obligation to use "sound experimentation and evaluation" procedures (Anderson and Ball, 1978; Riecken and Boruch, 1974). Were methods with known biases used? Did an adequate number of students participate? Was an appropriate analytical model used? Were the limitations of the results admitted? Were the objectives assessed as stated? Validity of the assessment methods will always be a paramount issue. Gender bias and racial or ethnic biases should be considered in the selection and design of methods, especially in general education.

In some cases, sources may be unaware of proper assessment procedures. In other cases, major problems at the institution are skirted because of a fear of results. Most of these problems can be prevented if a wide array of participants is involved in the efforts. It is also helpful to include outside consultants to review procedures and techniques and to contribute other ideas.

Finally, departments and institutions have an obligation to keep student data confidential and to report individual information back to the student. Unless permission is secured beforehand, students are protected by the Buckley Amendment (the Family Educational Rights and Privacy Act of 1974) from public release of identifiable assessment data. Some institutions collect data anonymously; however, this practice weakens assessment studies because such data cannot be linked to other available information about a particular student. For example, it is useful to compare test scores with courses completed, but such comparisons cannot be made unless individual test takers can be identified.

When assessment data are reported back to students after scoring, they learn from the assessment experience itself. Moreover, the assessment program is strengthened, since students who feel a part of assessment and who receive feedback are likely to take assessment more seriously.

One major problem with individual assessment reporting is that it requires considerable time and financial resources. Assessment information can be reported back through courses or through the advising programs. Longwood College in Virginia trains undergraduates to report information to their peers. Often, individual written score reports can be transmitted along with information about designated campus locations where further explanation can be obtained.

Institutions should make clear at the outset that students are required to participate in assessment activities. Statements about students' responsibilities should be included in the institution's catalogue and announced at convenient times—for instance, at orientation sessions for new students. To avoid confusion, an institution might have entering students read or sign a statement acknowledging that assessment is required. An example of such a statement is given in Chapter Two.

Issues of ethics also extend to faculty, who may feel that assessment can intrude into their academic freedom. On the one hand, faculty have a responsibility to teach what is stated in institutional and program objectives. For instance, if the "scientific method" is included as an objective under a general studies natural science distribution requirement, the instructors in all such courses (that is, general studies courses in geology, biology, physics, chemistry, and astronomy) will be expected to teach the scientific method. On the other hand, the objectives of any program should be determined by the faculty and student affairs staff, not by state officials. To avoid the imposition of statewide course requirements, such as those mandated for kindergarten through twelfth-grade levels, faculty will undoubtedly be motivated to state their own educational objectives and methods.

Conclusion

This chapter has explained the importance of the source, the channel or mode, the message communicated, and the audience for the assessment information, or *who* says *what* and *how* to *whom*. These four perspectives are important because the mere collection and interpretation of results does not guarantee that any *action* will be taken. Successful assessment efforts culminate in the use of the information for decision making. The final section of the chapter, addressing the ethical considerations of assessment reporting and uses, is meant to emphasize the importance of data accuracy, quality, and confidentiality.

NINE

The Promise of Assessment for Improving Educational Quality

 This chapter reviews some of the major issues covered earlier, explains how to organize the campus for assessment, and discusses emerging issues and new roles for assessment in higher education.

In the preceding chapters, the assessment steps are covered in a specific order: establishing objectives, selecting assessment methods, designing assessment methods, collecting assessment information, analyzing assessment information, and reporting and using assessment information. (This process can be repeated as data suggest new objectives or new questions to be asked and explored.) These steps are eventually addressed in most assessment programs, but not necessarily in the sequence presented here. Consequently, educators who skip the first step and hastily select and administer a proprietary examination from a testing organization will soon ask what the data mean. If program objectives and performance expectations are not clearly expressed beforehand, the sole accumulation of data may mean little. When student information is collected in this way, it rarely proves useful in decision making.

In addition, the various steps must be explored carefully and completely. Otherwise, the resulting information will not aid decision-making processes. In some institutions, for instance, clear program objectives do not exist beyond the vague, general goal statements. If, instead, discussions about what to assess resulted in

linearity

the formulation of specific objectives, they would throw light on what to teach as well. Similarly, most principles of instrument selection and design also can be applied to classroom and student affairs programs. One of the best ways to improve instruction is to improve classroom testing procedures. The other assessment steps—collecting, analyzing, and using assessment information—can help us understand how students learn and develop. Changes in students' ways of thinking, doing, and feeling do not generally come about with the completion of a single course or a student affairs workshop. It may be a combination of experiences within and outside the classroom that best produces positive change in students' lives. Serious assessment programs will be committed to long-time searches for the campus environmental influences that work best.

Because assessment has received attention as an entity in itself, some educators have mistakenly established assessment programs that operate independently—apart from the regular curriculum and program discussions on individual campuses. But when assessment is structured as a stand-alone process, it will be targeted for criticism and will die. If an institution considers the assessment process as a means, not an end, then discussions about program quality will be hard to separate from discussions about instructional methods, curricula, programs, and services. An assessment program will remain alive and will flourish only if the principles of assessment are integrated into educational decision-making processes.

Organizing the Campus for Assessment

Most institutions begin assessment by convening a campus-wide assessment committee to make recommendations about what to do. The members of this committee usually study other institutions that have successful assessment programs, invite outside consultants to outline key issues, and attend some kind of assessment conference, such as the American Association for Higher Education's annual Assessment Forum.

Among the issues confronted by these campus-wide assessment committees, foremost is the matter of faculty involvement. Faculty want to ensure that assessment is in their control, and most administrators and state agencies really want the faculty to assume the responsibility for producing viable, defensible assessment information. But faculty often complain that they cannot work unless released time is provided or they are in some other way compensated for the work involved in assessment. They may also protest that such work takes time away from their research. Since assessment, of course, focuses on instruction, this protest is really a version of the instruction-versus-research argument (Grassmuck, 1990). Unfortunately, this debate produces other potentially damaging comparisons—for instance, between research universities and liberal arts colleges or comprehensive schools. What is often lost sight of is the national cry of legislators for a renewed emphasis on instruction, not for the elimination or reduction of research studies. Also ignored is the fact that assessment is actually a reseach model about instruction. Are faculty's hypotheses about their students supported with data?

The campus-wide assessment committee will usually have several other questions to consider. First, how comprehensive will assessment be? Should it include student affairs as well as academic programs? In the past, student affairs units were excluded, but now the trend is to include them. Second, what will be assessed? This question often leads to the formation of other committees or the transfer of assessment responsibilities from the campus-wide committee to an existing committee. For instance, major program assessment may be decentralized to the departments; an alumni survey subcommittee may be formed to construct a survey; and general education responsibilities may be referred to an existing curriculum committee. Other subcommittees might include a basic skills committee or an affective development committee. Sometimes, specific areas or topics—such as computing literacy, information and learning resources, or writing—are referred to special committees or task forces for further definition and method design.

Third, who will coordinate assessment? This is a particularly tricky question for both the community colleges and the large universities. On many campuses, the vice president or dean for academic affairs typically has overall responsibility for assessment. On other campuses, assessment committees and personnel report to the vice president for student affairs or to the president. If assessment is comprehensive, including both student and academic affairs, then the assessment personnel logically report to the president of the institution.

Fourth, who will conduct the day-to-day assessment activities? On many campuses, a faculty member who is trained in measurement is given assessment responsibilities. If a campus does not have someone with this expertise, it may create a new position and hire someone with the technical expertise needed. When someone is brought in from the outside or from another part of the campus, this person will need to reassure the resident faculty that he or she does not pose a threat to them but, instead, can be a source of support. As was pointed out at the beginning of this book, the practice of assessment is both an art and a science.

The person or persons selected for day-to-day coordination will consult with the departments and will also perform other tasks not clearly associated with any organizational unit, such as surveying alumni about general institutional issues outside the major and, as the program matures, determining how the assessment information will be stored and maintained for future use and comparisons.

The most labor-intensive part of the assessment process takes place at the beginning stages. After a unit has established its objectives and adopted its assessment methods, what follows is usually fine-tuning of those objectives and methods. And after data are collected, the most interesting aspects of assessment usually follow for faculty and staff. When results are available, even the most skeptical staff will want to review and speculate about interpretations.

Here are some suggestions for assessment coordinators who are in the process of establishing an assessment program:

1. Do not start every program at the same time.
2. Choose people who are enthusiastic about the process and let them report their success to colleagues.
3. Remember that assessment (that is, the process of determining what has contributed to students' learning and development) is a very complex endeavor. The further faculty and staff move from assessing specific areas, such as knowledge achievement, to assessing more abstract areas, such as reasoning, the more difficult it becomes to prove institutional impact. Some staff

will claim, and appropriately so, that some outcomes cannot be measured until the graduate has left the institution and entered society. However, the further the student is from the educational experience, the harder it is to attribute those outcomes to the educational institution's influence.

4. Although specific subject matter knowledge and skills are important, also consider assessing personal development. As was discussed earlier, cognitive and affective developmental changes are usually more long lasting than specific knowledge.

Emerging Issues

One of the difficulties in assessment is that knowledge is rapidly expanding, so that new information is constantly being produced and some older information is becoming obsolete. Faculty in computing science departments, for example, are reluctant to specify subject matter content objectives in their field, since that content can become obsolete in just a few years. Instead, some computing science programs have chosen to state their objectives so that they reflect the rapidly increasing knowledge in their fields. For instance, students may be expected to "pick up a description of a new programming language and write a program in it." Such objectives do not specify that certain computer programming languages should be learned, because new languages frequently appear and old ones become obsolete. Therefore, the new objectives concentrate on developing the student's ability to solve a problem, rather than on teaching a specific way to solve a problem.

With increasing knowledge, new subdivisions have appeared within a particular discipline (Resnick and Goulden, 1987). Is it reasonable to expect students to be competent in all of these subfields? Consider the major of communications. Subfields of journalism, telecommunication, corporate media, visual communication, alternative dispute resolution, interpersonal communication, organizational communication, and public relations now exist. Should communication majors be assessed in all these areas or in just one or two? More generally, how many objectives can be specified for our intended graduates? In this time of specialization, is it reasonable to expect common competencies for all graduates? The assessment process brings problems such as these to light.

Another issue in assessment will remain ever present: a concern about the quality of information used to make decisions about students and programs. In the past, rapidly increasing enrollments led to an emphasis on accommodating greater numbers of students. Allocation of monies was naturally based on the number of students. The lack of qualitative indices for program review became more evident, however, when retrenchment was necessary at some institutions; that is, it was difficult to determine what to cut. Now that these institutions do not have to adjust to rapidly increasing enrollments, perhaps they can improve their existing programs. For example, the University of Tennessee at Knoxville reduced enrollment without an accompanying budget reduction and emphasized self-improvement through its assessment program. Educators often lament the fact that budgets are driven by "bean-counting" exercises of FTE and space utilization reports. More direct measures of quality (such as student learning and development information) have at least an equal place among other data used in the decision-making process.

Ewell (1990a) provides an extension of this argument in his review of assessment policies across the United States. He believes that assessment should be viewed as an "opportunity" for securing further advantage with political constituents. According to Ewell, educators have too often viewed assessment as a compliance exercise when outside intrusion was feared. Such fears of educational intrusion by politicians are largely unfounded in areas of institutional autonomy or academic freedom. Nor did assessment turn out to be a "disguised retrenchment device" (Ewell, 1990a, p. 5). In fact, the opposite is true. From an external constituent perspective, the *lack* of an institutional assessment program prohibits further budgeting expansion. Therefore, those who balk at "greater accountability" are, in fact, "missing a major opportunity."

Another emerging issue concerns the role of the division of student affairs in higher education and in assessment (Mable, 1988). Does student affairs contribute to the direct educational mission of the institution, or is it just a support service? Do student affairs staff directly influence students' development? If they do, they should be involved in the assessment process. For some divisions of student affairs, this decision is easy: either development is part of a mission or it is not. For student affairs groups at other institutions, the choice is less clear. The assessment process will help to clarify the direction and functions of the student affairs profession as a whole.

Another issue relates to the way that assessment information is collected. Traditionally, institutions have relied on selected-response formats, particularly multiple-choice tests. The need to tailor an assessment method to a particular institution supports the use of alternative methods for assessment in higher education. College faculty are comfortable with using ratings of essays, problems, class projects, presentations, and similar products and performances. For these reasons, the use of ratings will continue to grow in popularity. Evidence of this trend also exists in the professions. For example, the education field is shifting from multiple-choice tests to observational ratings of teaching style (Shulman, 1987); the American Assembly of Collegiate Schools of Business (1987) has sponsored the design of rating procedures for a variety of personal characteristics; and ratings about "habits of mind" have always been emphasized in the humanities. To meet these needs, new technical improvements in the design of rating scales will follow in the field of measurement.

As higher education continues to develop its assessment programs, institutions will begin to discover which current practices are more effective than others. As evidence becomes available about effectiveness or lack of it, certain practices may be retired. Institutions will discover what is worth financing and what is not. Faculty will determine which teaching methods work best with particular students (Cross, 1990).

As our definitions of education become sharper, they will become clearer to those outside of higher education as well. How well does the general public understand what a "liberally educated person" is? As Ewell (1989) points out, the public's lack of understanding about higher education translates into lower financial support in the public sector. Institutions that are unclear about their educational objectives may also have unclear commitments about teaching. When they are encouraged to clarify these objectives, the uniqueness of each institution, both public and private, will be more apparent.

Another change that will emerge at many institutions is a greater degree of cooperation among academic departments as well as between academic faculty and student affairs staff. When faculty begin to understand how and why students change, they will also begin to view responsibility for education as a shared venture rather than isolated in a single department or in a single course. In general education, for example, writing ability is not developed solely through composition courses. Appreciation of the arts is developed not only from coursework but also from participation in out-of-class fine-arts activities. And complex abilities, such as cognitive reasoning, may emerge only after a series of events in the student's life extending beyond just one semester.

A last issue that awaits assessment has to do with the increasing diversity in our colleges and universities (Levine and Associates, 1989). Large numbers of students and staff representing different ethnic and cultural backgrounds, life-styles, and ages will continue to appear on our campuses. This diversity should prompt educators to reconsider their evaluation practices. As a caution, institutions should make comparisons between white students and minority students only when a particular reason or question exists. Why compare African-American and white students on existing test information? Why compare Hispanics and white students on methods in the major? Unless some reason exists to do so, any differences found might lead to erroneous conclusions and prove damaging. Instead, it might be more useful to examine differences within an ethnic or racial group. Why did some Asian students learn more than other Asian students? As was discussed in Chapters Four and Five, the assessment method that is selected or designed must be carefully checked for validity, so that acute biases that distort group differences are eliminated. Moreover, instruments should continue to be updated as we learn more about the educational development of minorities and other groups.

Diversity and assessment might seem, at first glance, to be strange bedfellows; actually, however, assessment can coexist with diversity quite comfortably as our institutions begin to accept increasing numbers of minorities from various ethnic groups or racial backgrounds. American education has always prided itself on the diversity of its institutions. Differences exist even among four-year public institutions in the same state. These institutions have resisted statewide testing efforts to conform to common outcomes because, they contend, their educational programs are unique. For example, not all institutions may claim to have the same major program in languages and literature. The differences become more pronounced in general education. As demographics change, institutions potentially could become even more unique as they appeal to various student ethnic or racial groups. One institution may develop specific objectives for reaching students from certain cultures. Another institution in the same state system or geographical region may set different goals for different cultures. When this scenario unfolds, the role of assessment will be to ensure that these unique goals are being met, rather than to draw distinctions among minority groups or among institutions.

This diversity also has implications beyond the classroom. Gross and Scott (1990) report that labor shortages will occur in the coming decade because of a scarcity in the traditional eighteen to thirty-four age group. To make up for this scarcity in the work force, workers representing nontraditional groups will be needed. And these workers will need to be trained not just in the vocational sense but in the intellectual sense of developing "habits of mind." Similarly, Levine and Associates (1989) have documented the shrinking pool of traditional-age students who might attend college. They predict that many colleges will increasingly be admitting the "underserved" student, who matriculates with greater academic and personal needs. As a result, there will be a continuing emphasis on basic skills assessment and on devising methods for helping "high-risk" students succeed. Entry-level assessment programs should not be limited to discovering basic skill deficiencies but should also determine other factors that contribute to college success or failure. For example, Buczynski and Erwin (1990) found that the metacognition skills of at-risk students who succeed are greater than those of at-risk students who fail. These underserved students also will require adequate personnel services, such as cocurricular programming, counseling, financial aid, health, and other support services, if they are to remain in school. Assessment can determine which student needs what kind of help. No longer can higher education afford all student services for everybody.

Again, it is easy to lapse into thinking that the only purpose of assessment is for accountability and for documenting the "return on investment" to legislators and the public (Ewell, 1990b). Although this purpose is important, the opportunity to establish the value of general education and of a "liberal arts education" is also of paramount importance. Higher education needs to be more clear about what education is, what it has to offer, and how it can help our society. As Cross (1990) reminds us, if something cannot be measured, it is less likely to be improved.

In the future, higher education may take a different perspective about accountability and assessment. Instead of viewing documentation of quality as a burdensome or threatening task, assessment may become a major tool for recovering, holding onto, or gaining new resources for the institution. In some states, higher education's alotted percentage of the state budget is declining, and the privileged position of higher education is under question. Competition for new monies and for students will remain keen. Assessment evidence might prove helpful for documenting the worth of higher education, and in some instances, the possible damage due to budget cuts.

In closing, I would like to remind educators that assessment is largely what we educators make it. We can decide whether to use assessment effectively and ethically or to resist requests for evaluation or to comply with such requests in a casual and uncommitted way. In the future, the ways that we practice assessment will inevitably change. New creations and innovations will make the approaches presented here obsolete. I hope that faculty and student development professionals will be the ones to determine this future. I hope that they will shape our educational practices so that they can point to the specific benefits our students receive as a result of their collegiate experiences.

RESOURCE A

Proficiency Guidelines for Rating a Student's Ability to Speak a Foreign Language

Novice	The Novice level is characterized by the ability to communicate minimally with learned material.
Novice-Low	Oral production consists of isolated words and perhaps a few high-frequency phrases. Essentially no functional communication ability.
Novice-Mid	Oral production continues to consist of isolated words and learned phrases within very predictable areas of need, although quantity is increased. Vocabulary is sufficient only for handling simple, elementary needs and expressing basic courtesies. Utterances rarely consist of more than two or three words and show frequent long pauses and repetition of interlocutor's words. Speaker may have some difficulty producing even the simplest utterances. Some Novice-Mid speakers will be understood only with great difficulty.
Novice-High	Able to satisfy partially the requirements of basic communicative exchanges by relying heavily on learned utterances but occasionally expanding these through simple recombinations of their elements. Can ask questions or make statements involving learned material. Shows signs of spontaneity although this falls short of real autonomy of expression. Speech continues to consists of learned utterances rather than of personalized, situationally adapted ones. Vocabulary centers on

Source: American Council on the Teaching of Foreign Languages, 1986. Reproduced by permission.

areas such as basic objects, places, and most common kinship terms. Pronunciation may still be strongly influenced by first language. Errors are frequent and, in spite of repetition, some Novice-High speakers will have difficulty being understood even by sympathetic interlocutors.

Intermediate

The Intermediate level is characterized by the speaker's ability to:
—create with the language by combining and recombining learned elements, though primarily in a reactive mode;
—initiate, minimally sustain, and close in a simple way basic communicative tasks; and
—ask and answer questions.

Intermediate-Low

Able to handle successfully a limited number of interactive, task-oriented, and social situations. Can ask and answer questions, initiate and respond to simple statements, and maintain face-to-face conversation, although in a highly restricted manner and with much linguistic inaccuracy. Within these limitations, can perform such tasks as introducing self, ordering a meal, asking directions, and making purchases. Vocabulary is adequate to express only the most elementary needs. Strong interference from native language may occur. Misunderstandings frequently arise, but with repetition, the Intermediate-Low speaker can generally be understood by sympathetic interlocutors.

Intermediate-Mid

Able to handle successfully a variety of uncomplicated, basic communicative tasks and social situations. Can talk simply about self and family members. Can ask and answer questions and participate in simple conversations on topics beyond the most immediate needs; e.g., personal history and leisure time activities. Utterance length increases slightly, but speech may continue to be characterized by frequent long pauses, since the smooth incorporation of even basic conversational strategies is often hindered as the speaker struggles to create appropriate language forms. Pronunciation may continue to be strongly influenced by first language and fluency may still be strained. Although misunderstandings still arise, the Intermediate-Mid speaker can generally be understood by sympathetic interlocutors.

Intermediate-High   Able to handle successfully most uncomplicated communicative tasks and social situations. Can initiate, sustain, and close a general conversation with a number of strategies appropriate to a range of circumstances and topics, but errors are evident. Limited vocabulary still necessitates hesitation and may bring about slightly unexpected circumlocution. There is emerging evidence of connected discourse, particularly for simple narration and/or description. The Intermediate-High speaker can generally be understood even by interlocutors not accustomed to dealing with speakers at this level, but repetition may still be required.

Advanced   The Advanced level is characterized by the speaker's ability to:
—converse in a clearly participatory fashion;
—initiate, sustain, and bring to closure a wide variety of communicative tasks, including those that require an increased ability to convey meaning with diverse language strategies due to a complication or an unforeseen turn of events;
—satisfy the requirements of school and work situations; and
—narrate and describe with paragraph-length connected discourse.

Able to satisfy the requirements of everyday situations and routine school and work requirements. Can handle with confidence but not with facility complicated tasks and social situations, such as elaborating, complaining, and apologizing. Can narrate and describe with some details, linking sentences together smoothly. Can communicate facts and talk casually about topics of current public and personal interest, using general vocabulary. Shortcomings can often be smoothed over by communicative strategies, such as pause fillers, stalling devices, and different rates of speech. Circumlocution which arises from vocabulary or syntactic limitations very often is quite successful, though some groping for words may still be evident. The Advanced-level speaker can be understood without difficulty by native interlocutors.

Advanced-Plus   Able to satisfy the requirements of a broad variety of everyday, school, and work situations. Can discuss concrete topics related to particular interests and special fields of competence. There is emerging evidence of ability to support opinions, explain in detail, and hypothesize. The Advanced-Plus speaker often shows a well developed ability to compensate for an imperfect grasp of some forms with confident use of communicative strategies, such as paraphrasing and circumlocution. Differentiated vocabulary and intonation are effectively used to communicate fine shades of meaning. The Advanced-Plus speaker often shows remarkable fluency and ease of speech but under the demands of Superior-level, complex tasks, language may break down or prove inadequate.

Superior

The Superior level is characterized by the speaker's ability to:
—participate effectively in most formal and informal conversations on practical, social, professional, and abstract topics;
—support opinions and hypothesize using native-like discourse strategies.
Able to speak the language with sufficient accuracy to participate effectively in most formal and informal conversations on practical, social, professional, and abstract topics. Can discuss special fields of competence and interest with ease. Can support opinions and hypothesize, but may not be able to tailor language to audience or discuss in depth highly abstract or unfamiliar topics. Usually the Superior-level speaker is only partially familiar with regional or other dialectical variants. The Superior-level speaker commands a wide variety of interactive strategies and shows good awareness of discourse strategies. The latter involves the ability to distinguish main ideas from supporting information through syntactic, lexical, and suprasegmental features (pitch, stress, intonation). Sporadic errors may occur, particularly in low-frequency structures and some complex high-frequency structures more common to formal writing, but no patterns of errors are evident. Errors do not disturb the native speaker or interfere with communication.

RESOURCE B

Alumni Questionnaire

INSTRUCTIONS: Please respond to the following JMU Alumni Questionnaire by marking your answers in No. 2 pencil on the accompanying blue answer sheet. Please write and fill in your name. Make sure that your answers correspond to the appropriate question number.

1. What was your year of graduation from JMU?

   1988 = A
   1987 = B
   1986 = C
   1985 = D
   1984 = E

2. Sex

   Female = A
   Male   = B

3. Race/Ethnic background:

   White, Caucasian = A
   Black   = B
   Hispanic   = C
   Oriental/Asian   = D
   Other   = E

4. What was your approximate final grade point average?

   2.0–2.4 = A
   2.5–2.9 = B
   3.0–3.4 = C
   3.5–4.0 = D

Source: James Madison University, 1987. Reproduced by permission.

5. During your time at JMU, would you classify yourself primarily as a resident or a commuter student?

    Resident = A,   Commuter = B.

6. Did you graduate with a double major?

    Yes = A,   No = B

7. Which of the following best describes what you are currently doing? (Include self-employment and military as "employed.")

    Employed full time   = A
    Employed part time   = B
    Unemployed and seeking employment   = C
    Caring for a home/family   = D
    Not employed and not seeking employment   = E

8. Which best describes your employer?

    Private enterprise, including self-employment   = A
    Educational institution or system   = B
    Federal government, including military   = C
    State or local government   = D
    Other   = E

Complete questions 9–16 *only* if you are currently employed.

9–14. Indicate your satisfaction with the following aspects of your present job.

    Very dissatisfied   = A   Satisfied   = C
    Dissatisfied   = B   Very satisfied = D

    9. Degree of challenge   12. Professional advancement
    10. Geographic location   13. Working conditions
    11. Compensation and   14. Career potential
         benefits

15. How satisfied are you with the way JMU prepared you for your present occupation?

Very dissatisfied	=	A
Dissatisfied	=	B
Satisfied	=	C
Very satisfied	=	D

16. How closely related is your current occupation to your major at JMU?

Slightly related	=	A
Moderately related	=	B
Highly related	=	C
Not related	=	D

17. Since graduating from JMU, have you taken courses at another college? (If NO, skip to question 21)

Yes = A,   No = B

18. What is the major reason you continued your education? (Choose only ONE)

To satisfy job/career requirements	=	A
To learn a new occupation	=	B
To obtain or maintain a license or certificate	=	C
For general self-improvement	=	D
Other	=	E

19. Since leaving JMU, have you completed courses *toward* any of the following degrees but not finished the degree?

Master's	=	A
Law	=	B
Medicine	=	C
Doctorate (Other than law or medicine)	=	D
Other degree and/or certificate	=	E

20. Have you completed any of the following degrees since leaving JMU?

Master's	=	A
Law	=	B
Medicine	=	C
Doctorate (Other than law or medicine)	=	D
Other degree and/or certificate	=	E

21. How satisfied are you with the way JMU prepared you for your additional college work?

Very dissatisfied	=	A
Dissatisfied	=	B
Satisfied	=	C
Very satisfied	=	D

22-26. Please rate your degree of satisfaction with the following.

22. Overall JMU experience	Very dissatisfied =	A
23. Experience in major department	Dissatisfied =	B
24. Counseling and Student Development Center	Satisfied =	C
	Very satisfied =	D
25. Career Planning and Placement Center	No basis to judge =	E
26. Academic advising		

27-48. How satisfied are you with JMU's contribution to your personal growth in each of the following areas?

Very dissatisfied	=	A	Satisfied	=	C
Dissatisfied	=	B	Very satisfied	=	D

27. Writing effectively
28. Understanding and applying mathematics in daily life
29. Defining and solving problems
30. Developing appreciation of the arts
31. Creative thinking
32. Making logical inferences based on assumptions
33. Speaking effectively

34. Maintaining your physical health
35. Appreciating your role as a citizen
36. Applying scientific methods and principles
37. Awareness of different cultures and ideas
38. Learning independently
39. Cooperating with others
40. Selecting personal goals
41. Developing self-reliance
42. Exercising initiative
43. Developing persistence
44. Developing leadership skills
45. Tolerating other points of view
46. Using word processing skills on a computer
47. Using data analysis applications on a computer
48. Ability to learn new computing programs and applications

Student Involvement Survey

Please use this form to indicate the activities you participated in during the past summer session, the past fall semester, and the current spring semester.

The activities you might have done are listed by topic areas. Please indicate the degree of your involvement in each activity. If you did not participate in a listed activity, *leave that answer space blank. Always select from the available choices only the one answer which gives your highest level of involvement.* Please mark your responses on your green answer sheet.

Topic Area: On-Campus Events

Section I

A Attended 1-3 times
B Attended 4-6 times
C Attended more than 6 times
D Minor participant

E Major participant
F Directed, managed, or organized
G Received national, state, or regional award

Line	*On-Campus Activities*
1	Plays
2	Lectures/speakers

Source: James Madison University, 1988. Reproduced by permission.

3   Special events (e.g., block shows, talent shows)
4   Dance performance
5   Art exhibits (e.g., galleries/museums)
6   Concerts
7   Bands
8   Forensics
9   Films

Topic Area: Clubs and Organizations

Section I

A Member
B Committee member
C Committee chair

D Officer
E Major officer
F Major campus leader

Line	*Activities*
10	Campus-affiliated religious organizations
11	Fraternities/sororities
12	Honorary organizations
13	Judicial Board/Honor Council
14	Political groups
15	Professional/departmental
16	Publications (e.g., *The Breeze, Bluestone*)
17	Service organizations (e.g., Circle K)
18	Student government association
19	University governance (JMU commissions and committees)
20	University programming
21	University housing position (e.g., Resident Advisor)
22	University committees

Topic Area: Sports

Section I

A Attended 1–3 games
B Attended 4–10 games
C Attended more than 20
   games

D Member
E Captain
F National, regional, or state
   award

Line	Activities
23	Intramural team
24	Intercollegiate team
25	Manager/trainer/assistant coach
26	Cheerleader
27	Spectator

Topic Area: Academic Experiences

Section I

A Attended 1–3 times
B Attended 4–6 times
C Attended more than 6 times
D Minor participant

E Major participant
F Directed, managed, or
   organized
G Received national, state, or
   regional award

Line	Activities
28	Studies abroad
29	Conferences/conventions
30	Nonrequired internships/practicums
31	Honors program

Analysis." In R. L. Thorndike (ed.), *Educational Measurement.* Washington, D.C.: American Council on Education, 1971.

Banta, T. W. "Use of Outcomes Information at the University of Tennessee, Knoxville." In P. T. Ewell (ed.), *Assessing Educational Outcomes.* New Directions for Institutional Research, no. 47. San Francisco: Jossey-Bass, 1985.

Banta, T. W., and Schneider, J. A. "Using Faculty-Developed Exit Examinations to Evaluate Academic Programs." *Journal of Higher Education,* 1988, *59,* 69–83.

Baxter-Magolda, M. "A Rater-Training Program for Assessing Intellectual Development on the Perry Scheme." *Journal of College Student Personnel,* 1987, *28,* 356–364.

Beeler, K. J. "Decision Support Systems and the Art of Enrollment Management." *NASPA Journal,* 1989, *26,* 242–247.

Belenky, M. F., Clinchy, B. M., Goldberger, N. R., and Tarule, J. M. *Women's Way of Knowing: The Development of Self, Voice, and Mind.* New York: Basic Books, 1986.

Berk, R. A. *Criterion-Referenced Measurement: The State of the Art.* Baltimore: Johns Hopkins University Press, 1978.

Berk, R. A., (ed.). *Performance Assessment: Methods and Applications.* Baltimore: Johns Hopkins University Press, 1986.

Bloom, B. (ed.). *Taxonomy of Educational Objectives.* Vol. 1: *Cognitive Domain.* New York: McKay, 1956.

Blumenstyk, G. "Diversity Is Keynote of States' Efforts to Assess Students' Learning." *Chronicle of Higher Education,* July 20, 1988, pp. A17–26.

Bok, D. *Higher Learning.* Cambridge, Mass.: Harvard University Press, 1986a.

Bok, D. "Toward Education of Quality." *Harvard Magazine,* May–June 1986b, pp. 49–64.

Boulard, G. A. "Higher-Education Commissioners Urge State Systems to Limit Tuition Raises and to Explain Costs to Public." *Chronicle of Higher Education,* Sept. 21, 1988. p. A31.

Bowen, H. R. *Investment in Learning: The Individual and Social Value of Higher Education.* San Francisco: Jossey-Bass, 1977.

Bowen, H. R. "The Reform of Undergraduate Education: Estimated Costs." Paper presented at Wiagspread Conference, Racine, Wis., 1985.

Boyer, C. M., Ewell, P. T., Finney, J. E., and Mingle, J. R. "Assessment and Outcomes Measurement: A View from the States." *AAHE Bulletin*, 1987, *39*, 8–12.

Braskamp, L. A., Brandenburg, D. C., and Ory, J. C. *Evaluating Teaching Effectiveness: A Practical Guide*. Newbury Park, Calif.: Sage, 1984.

Braskamp, L. A., Brown, R. D., and Newman, D. L. "The Credibility of a Local Educational Program Evaluation Report: Author Source and Client Audience Characteristics." *American Educational Research Journal*, 1978, *15* (5), 441–450.

Bray, D. W. "The Management Process Study." *American Psychologist*, 1964, *19*, 419–429.

Bray, D. W. "The Assessment Center and the Study of Lives." *American Psychologist*, 1982, *37*, 180–189.

Brennan, R. L. "A Generalized Upper-Lower Item Discrimination Index." *Educational and Psychological Measurement*, 1972, *32*, 289–303.

Brennan, R. L. *Elements of Generalizability Theory*. Iowa City: American College Testing Program, 1983.

Brinkerhoff, R. O., Brethower, D. M., Hluchkyj, T., and Nowakowski, J. R. *Program Evaluation: A Practitioner's Guide for Trainers and Educators*. Boston: Kluwer-Nijhoff, 1983.

Brown, F. G. *Principles of Educational and Psychological Testing*. New York: Holt, Rhinehart & Winston, 1976.

Brown, R. D. "How Evaluation Can Make a Difference." In G. R. Hanson (ed.), *Evaluating Program Effectiveness*. New Directions for Student Services, no. 1. San Francisco: Jossey-Bass, 1978.

Brown, R. D., Braskamp, L. A., and Newman, D. L. "Evaluator Credibility and Acceptance as a Function of Report Styles: Do Jargon and Data Make a Difference?" *Evaluation Quarterly*, 1978, *2* (2), 331–341.

Brown, R. D., Newman, D. L., and Rivers, L. S. "Perceived Need for Evaluation and Data Usage as Influences on an Evaluation's Impact on Decision Making." *Educational Evaluation and Policy Analysis*, 1980, *2*, 67–72.

Brown, R. D., Newman, D. L., and Rivers, L. S. "Does Superintendent's Opinion Affect School Boards' Evaluation Information

Needs? An Empirical Investigation." *Urban Education,* 1985, *20* (20), 204–221.

Buczynski, P. L. and Erwin, T. D. "Who's 'At-Risk'? Can Assessment Help?" Paper presented at the Fifth American Association for Higher Education Conference on Assessment in Higher Education, Washington, D.C., June 1990.

Bull, K. S., and Newman, D. L. "The Effect of Audience Role and Decision Context on School Evaluation Information Needs." *Journal of Research and Development in Education,* 1986, *1* (2), 28–36.

Cameron, L., Chappell, M. A., and Riordan, D. "Table of Specification for Library Competencies in the Major of English." Unpublished report, James Madison University, Harrisonburg, Va., 1989.

Campbell, D. T. "Reforms as Experiments." *American Psychologist,* 1969, *24,* 409–429.

Campbell, D. T., and Fiske, D. W. "Convergent and Discriminant Validation by the Multitrait-Multimethod Matrix." *Psychological Bulletin,* 1959, *56,* 81–105.

Campbell, D. T., and Stanley, J. C. *Experimental and Quasi-Experimental Designs for Research.* Skokie, Ill.: Rand McNally, 1966.

Carter, R. K. "Client Reactions to Negative Findings and the Latent Conservative Function of Evaluation Studies." *American Sociologist,* 1971, *6,* 118–124.

Chickering, A. W. *Education and Identity.* San Francisco: Jossey-Bass, 1969.

Choppin, B. H. "Evaluation, Assessment, and Measurement." Topic review in T. Husen and T. N. Postelethwaite (eds.), *The International Encyclopedia of Education Research and Studies.* Vol. 3, pp. 1747–1748. Elmsford, N.Y.: Pergamon Press, 1985.

Coffman, W. E. "Essay Examination." In R. L. Thorndike (ed.), *Educational Measurement.* Washington, D.C.: American Council on Education, 1971.

Colby, A., Kohlberg, L., Gibbs, J., and Lieberman, M. "A Longitudinal Study of Moral Judgment." *Monographs of the Society for Research in Child Development,* 1983, *48,* serial no. 200.

Cole, N. S., and Moss, P. A. "Bias in Test Use." In R. L. Linn (ed.), *Educational Measurement*. New York: Macmillan, 1989.

College Board. *Technical Manual for the Field Test of Computerized Placement Tests, Version 3.0: Featuring the College-Level Mathematics Test and Seamless Serial Testing*. New York: College Board, 1990.

Committee to Develop Standards for Educational and Psychological Testing. *Standards for Educational and Psychological Testing*. Washington, D.C.: American Psychological Association, 1985.

Conoley, J. C., and O'Neil, H. F., Jr. "A Primer for Developing Test Items." In H. F. O'Neil, Jr. (ed.), *Procedures for Instructional Systems Development*. San Diego, Calif: Academic Press, 1979.

Cook, T. D., Leviton, L. C., and Shadish, W. R. "Program Evaluation." In G. Lindzey and E. Aronson (eds.), *Handbook of Social Psychology*. New York: Random House, 1985.

Cook, T. D., and Shadish, W. R. "Metaevaluation: An Evaluation of the Congressionally-Mandated Evaluation System for Community Mental Health Centers." In G. Stahler and W. R. Tash (eds.), *Innovative Approaches to Mental Health Evaluation*. San Diego, Calif.: Academic Press, 1982.

Cook, T. D., and Shadish, W. R. "Program Evaluation: The Worldly Science." *Annual Review in Psychology*, 1986, *37* 193–232.

Cooperman, S., Bloom, J., and Bloom, D. S. *The Registered Holistic Scoring Method for Scoring Student Essays: Scoring Guide for Training*. Trenton: New Jersey State Department of Education, 1983.

Cox, C. "Quality—JMU Group Seeks to Diagnose Needs for Next Century." *Richmond Times Dispatch*, Jan. 5, 1986, p. 1.

Cox, R. C., and Vargas, J. S. "A Comparison of Item Selection Techniques for Norm-Referenced and Criterion-Referenced Tests." Paper presented at annual meeting of the National Council on Measurement in Education, Chicago, Feb. 1966.

Crocker, L., and Algina, J. *Introduction to Classical and Modern Test Theory*. New York: Holt, Rinehart & Winston, 1986.

Cronbach, L. J. "Coefficient Alpha and the Internal Structure of Tests." *Psychometrika*, 1951, *16*, 297–334.

Cronbach, L. J., and others. *Toward Reform of Program Evaluation: Aims, Methods, and Institutional Arrangements.* San Francisco: Jossey-Bass, 1980.

Cross, K. P. "Collaborative Classroom Assessment." Keynote address at the Fifth American Association for Higher Education Conference on Assessment in Higher Education, Washington, D.C., June 30, 1990.

Cross, K. P., and Angelo, T. A. *Classroom Assessment Techniques.* Ann Arbor, Mich.: National Center for Research to Improve Teaching, 1988.

Dalton, J. "Physical Education and Recreation Assessment Report." Unpublished report, James Madison University, Harrisonburg, Va., 1989.

Daughdrill, J. H. "Assessment Is Doing More for Higher Education Than Any Other Development in Recent History." *Chronicle of Higher Education,* Jan. 27, 1988, p. A52.

Denzin, N. K. *The Research Act.* New York: McGraw-Hill, 1978.

Dressel, P. L., and Associates. *Evaluation in Higher Education.* Boston: Houghton Mifflin, 1961.

Ebel, R. L. *Essentials of Educational Measurement.* (3rd ed.) Englewood Cliffs, N.J. Prentice-Hall, 1979.

Edgerton, R. "An Assessment of Assessment." In *Assessing the Outcomes of Higher Education.* Proceedings of the 1986 ETS Invitational Conference. Princeton, N.J.: Educational Testing Service, 1987.

Educational Testing Service. *Major Field Achievement Tests: Pilot Year Program Manual.* Princeton, N.J.: Educational Testing Service, 1988.

Educational Testing Service. *Comparative Data Guide for 1990–91.* Princeton, N.J.: Educational Testing Service, 1990.

Erickson, R. C., and Wentling, T. L. *Measuring Student Growth: Techniques and Procedures for Occupational Education.* Newton, Mass.: Allyn & Bacon, 1976.

Erwin, T. D. "The Influence of Roommate Assignments upon Students' Maturity." *Research in Higher Education,* 1983a, *19,* 451–459.

Erwin, T. D. "The Scale of Intellectual Development: Measuring

Perry's Scheme." *Journal of College Student Personnel*, 1983b, *24*, 6-12.

Erwin, T. D. "Students' Contribution to Their College Costs and Intellectual Development." *Research in Higher Education*, 1986, *25*, 194-203.

Erwin, T. D., and Delworth, U. "An Instrument to Measure Chickering's Vector of Identity." *NASPA Journal*, 1980, *17*, 19-24.

Erwin, T. D., and Delworth, U. "Formulating Environmental Constructs That Affect Students' Identity." *NASPA Journal*, 1982, *20*, 47-55.

Erwin, T. D., and Love, W. B. "Selected Environmental Factors Associated with Change in Students' Development." *NASPA Journal*, 1989, *26*, 256-264.

Erwin, T. D., Menard, A. J., and Scott, R. L. "Student Development Outcome Assessment: A Model for Beginning." Paper presented at annual meeting of the American College Personnel Association, Miami, March 1988.

Erwin, T. D., and Miller, S. W. "Technology and the Three R's." *NASPA Journal*, 1985, *22*, 47-51.

Erwin, T. D., and Tollefson, A. L. "A Data Base Management Model for Student Development." *Journal of College Student Personnel*, 1982, *23*, 70-76.

Ewell, P. T. *Information on Student Outcomes: How to Get It and How to Use It.* Boulder, Colo.: National Center for Higher Education Management Systems, 1984.

Ewell, P. T. (ed.). *Assessing Educational Outcomes.* New Directions for Institutional Research, no. 47. San Francisco: Jossey-Bass, 1985.

Ewell, P. T. "Assessment: Where Are We?" *Change*, 1987, *19*, 23-28.

Ewell, P. T. "Implementing Assessment: Some Organizational Issues." In T. W. Banta (ed.), *Implementing Outcomes Assessment: Promise and Perils.* New Directions for Institutional Research, no. 59. San Franciso: Jossey-Bass, 1988a.

Ewell, P. T. "Outcomes, Assessment, and Academic Improvement: In Search of Usable Knowledge." In J. C. Smart (ed.), *Higher Education: Handbook of Theory and Research.* New York: Agatha Press, 1988b.

Ewell, P. T. "Hearts and Minds: Some Reflections on the Ideologies on Assessment." Paper presented at the Fourth American Association for Higher Education Conference on Assessment in Higher Education, Atlanta, June 1989.

Ewell, P. T. "Assessment and the 'New Accountability': A Guide for Policy." Unpublished paper, National Center for Higher Education Management Systems, 1990a.

Ewell, P. T. "Assessment and the New Accountability: What Do They Want From Us, Really?" Paper presented at the Fifth American Association for Higher Education Conference on Assessment in Higher Education, Washington, D.C., June 1990b.

Ewell, P. T., Finney, J. E., and Lenth, C. "Filling in the Mosaic: Emerging Patterns of State Based Assessment." *AAHE Bulletin*, April 1990, *42*, 3–5.

Ewell, P. T., and Jones, D. P. "The Costs of Assessment." In C. Adelman (ed.), *Assessment in American Higher Education: Issues and Contexts*. Washington, D.C.: U.S. Government Printing Office, 1985.

Ewell, P. T., Parker, R., and Jones, D. P. *Establishing a Longitudinal Student Tracking System: An Implementation Handbook*. Boulder, Colo.: National Center for Higher Education Management Systems, 1988.

Farmer, D. W. *Enhancing Student Learning: Emphasizing Essential Competencies in Academic Progress*. Wilkes-Barre, Pa.: King's College Press, 1988.

Feldman, K. A., and Newcomb, T. M. *The Impact of College on Students*. San Francisco: Jossey-Bass, 1969.

Feldt, L. S., and Brennan, R. L. "Reliability." In R. L. Linn (ed.), *Educational Measurement*. New York: Macmillan, 1989.

Finlayson, D. S. "The Reliability of the Marking of Essays." *British Journal of Educational Psychology*, 1951, *21*, 126–143.

Finn, C. E., Jr. "U.S. Campuses Are Bursting at the Quads." *Wall Street Journal*, Jan. 27, 1988, p. 24.

Fishbein, M., and Ajzen, I. *Belief, Attitudes, Intention and Behavior: An Introduction to Theory and Research*. Reading, Mass.: Addison-Wesley, 1975.

Fiske, D. W. (ed.). *Problems with Language Imprecision*. New Directions for Methodology of Social and Behavioral Science, no. 9. San Francisco: Jossey-Bass, 1981.

Fiske, E. B. "Colleges Prodded to Prove Worth—React to Pressures to Assess the Effects of Education." *New York Times,* Jan. 18, 1987, p. 27.

Fitzpatrick, R., and Morrison, E. J. "Performance and Product Evaluation." In R. L. Thorndike (ed.), *Educational Measurement.* Washington, D.C.: American Council on Education, 1971.

Flanagan, J. C. "The Critical Incident Technique." *Psychological Bulletin,* 1954, *51,* 327–355.

Fogli, L., Hulin, C. L., and Blood, M. R. "Development of First-Level Behavioral Job Criteria." *Journal of Applied Psychology,* 1971, *55,* 3–8.

Fong, B. "The External Examiner Approach to Assessment." Paper presented at the Second American Association for Higher Education Conference on Assessment in Higher Education, Denver, June 1987.

Forrest, A. "Evaluating the Practicality of General Education." *North Central Association Quarterly,* 1979, *53,* 420–427.

Forrest, A., and Steele, J. M. *College Outcome Measures Project: Defining and Measuring General Education Knowledge and Skills.* Iowa City: American College Testing Program, 1982.

Frederiksen, N. "Proficiency Tests for Training Evaluation." In R. Glaswer (ed.), *Training Research and Education.* New York: Wiley, 1965.

Frederiksen, N., Saunders, D. R., and Wand, B. "The In-Basket Test." *Psychological Monographs,* 1957, *71,* (9, whole no. 438).

Gabbin, A. L., and Erwin, T. D. "Monitoring the Quality of Accounting Programs: Current Initiatives and Future Directions of Student Outcome Assessment." Unpublished paper, 1990.

Gable, R. K. *Instrument Development in the Affective Domain.* Boston: Kluwer-Nijhoff, 1986.

Gardiner, L. F. *Planning for Assessment: Mission Statements, Goals, and Objectives.* Trenton: New Jersey Department of Higher Education, 1989.

Geis, G. L. (ed.). *Designing More Effective College Instruction.* Ann Arbor: Center for Research on Learning and Teaching, University of Michigan, 1970.

Glaser, E. M., and Taylor, S. H. "Factors Influencing the Success of Applied Research." *American Psychologist*, 1973, *28* (2), 140–146.

Glaser, R., and Klaus, D. "Proficiency Measurement: Assessing Human Performance." In R. M. Gagne (ed.), *Psychological Principles in System Development*. New York: Holt, Rinehart & Winston, 1963.

Glass, G. V. "Standards and Criteria." *Journal of Educational Measurement*, 1978, *15*, 237–261.

Glassboro College. "Progress Report on Institutional Goals and Assessment for Student Development." Unpublished manuscript, Glassboro, N.J., Office of Assessment, 1989.

Goldenson, R. M. *Longman Dictionary of Psychology and Psychiatry*. New York: Longman, 1984.

Goldman, R. D., and Slaughter, R. E. "Why College Grade Point Average Is Difficult to Predict." *Journal of Educational Psychology*, 1976, *68*, 9–14.

Grandy, J. "Models for Developing Computer-Based Indicators of College Student Learning in Computer Science." In C. Adelman (ed.), *Signs and Traces*. Washington, D.C.: U.S. Government Printing Office, 1989.

Grassmuck, K. "Some Research Universities Contemplate Sweeping Changes, Ranging from Management and Tenure to Teaching Methods." *Chronicle of Higher Education*, 1990, *37*, A1, A29–A30.

Gray, P. J. "Campus Profiles." In T. Banta (ed.), *Assessment Update: Progress, Trends, and Practices in Higher Education*, no. 1. San Francisco: Jossey-Bass, 1989.

Griffin, T. "The Physical Environment of the College Classroom and Its Effects on Students." *Campus Ecologist*, 1990, *8*, 1–4.

Gronlund, N. E. *Constructing Achievement Tests*. Englewood Cliffs, N.J.: Prentice-Hall, 1968.

Gross, D. M., and Scott, S. "Proceeding with Caution." *Time*, July 16, 1990, pp. 56–62.

Guba, E. G. "Problems in Utilizing the Results of Evaluation." *Journal of Research and Development in Education*, 1975, *8*, 42–54.

Guba, E. G., and Lincoln, Y. S. *Effective Evaluation: Improving the*

Usefulness of Evaluation Results Through Responsive and Naturalistic Approaches. San Francisco: Jossey-Bass, 1981.

Guion, R. M. "On Trinitarian Conceptions of Validity." *Professional Psychology*, 1980, *11*, 385–398.

Hakel, M. D. "Employment Interviewing." In K. M. Rowland and G. R. Ferris (eds.), *Personnel Management.* Newton, Mass.: Allyn & Bacon, 1982.

Halput, H. P. "Communications as a Basic Tool in Promoting Utilization of Research Findings." *Community Mental Health Journal*, 1966, *2* (3), 231–236.

Hambleton, R. K. (ed.). *Applications of Item Response Theory.* Vancouver: Educational Research Institute of British Columbia, 1983.

Hambleton, R. K., Swaminathan, J., Algina, J., and Coulson, D. B. "Criterion-Referenced Testing and Measurement: A Review of Technical Issues and Developments." *Review of Educational Research*, 1978, *48*, 1–47.

Hanson, G. R. (ed.). *Measuring Student Development.* New Directions for Student Services, no. 20. San Francisco: Jossey-Bass, 1982.

Hanson, G. R., and Lenning, O. T. "Evaluation of Student Development Programs." In G. E. Kuh (ed.), *Evaluation in Student Affairs.* Cincinnati: ACPA Media, University of Cincinnati, 1979.

Hartog, P., and Rhodes, E. C. *The Marks of Examiners.* New York: Macmillan, 1936.

Heath, D. H. *Growing Up in College: Liberal Education and Maturity.* San Francisco: Jossey-Bass, 1968.

Heath, D. H. *Maturity and Competence: A Transcultural View.* New York: Gardner Press, 1977.

Hogan, R., and Nicholson, R. A. "The Meaning of Personality Test Scores." *American Psychologist*, 1988, *43*, 621–626.

Hood, A. B. (ed.). *The Iowa Student Development Inventories.* Iowa City: Hitech Press, 1986.

House, E. R. *The Logic of Evaluative Argument.* CSE Monograph Series. Los Angeles: Graduate School, University of California, 1977.

House, E. R. *Evaluating with Validity.* Newbury Park, Calif.: Sage, 1980.

Houston, J. P. *Fundamentals of Learning.* San Diego, Calif.: Academic Press, 1976.

Hudgins, C. L. "Assessment Outcomes in the Humanities." Paper presented at the Second Annual Conference on Undergraduate Student Assessment of the State Council of Higher Education in Virginia and the Virginia Assessment Group, Richmond, 1988.

Hutchings, P. *Six Stories: Implementing Successful Assessment.* Paper presented at the Second American Association for Higher Education Conference on Assessment in Higher Education, Denver, 1987.

Hutchings, P. "Assessment and the Way We Work." Closing plenary address at the Fifth American Association for Higher Education Conference on Assessment in Higher Education, Washington, D.C., June 30, 1990.

Huynh, H. "Statistical Consideration of Mastery Scores." *Psychometrika,* 1976, *41,* 65–78.

Hyman, R., Jamison, A., Woodard, D. B., Jr., and Destinon, M. *Student Outcomes Assessment Survey, 1987–88.* Washington, D.C.: National Association of Student Personnel Administrators, 1988.

Jacob, P. I. *Changing Values in College: An Exploratory Study of the Impact of College Teaching.* New York: Harper & Row, 1957.

Jaeger, R. M. "A Proposal for Setting a Standard on the North Carolina High School Competency Test." Paper presented at the spring meeting of the North Carolina Association of Research in Education, Chapel Hill, 1978.

Joint Committee on Standards for Educational Evaluation. *Standards for Evaluation of Educational Programs, Projects, and Materials.* New York: McGraw-Hill, 1981.

Kean College. *A Proposal for Program Assessment at Kean College of New Jersey.* Union, N.J.: Kean College, 1986.

Kelly, D. "Value: The Final Exam Is the Toughest, Just What You Learned?" *USA Today,* Jan. 19, 1990, p. 3E.

Kleiman, L. S., and Faley, R. H. "The Implications of Professional and Legal Guidelines for Court Decisions Involving Criterion-Related Validity: A Review and Analysis." *Personnel Psychology,* 1985, *38,* 803–833.

Kohlberg, L. "Development of Moral Character and Moral Ideology." In M. L. Hoffman and L. W. Hoffman (eds.), *Review of Child Development Research.* Vol. 1. New York: Russell Sage Foundation, 1964.

Kroenke, D., and Dolan, K. *Business Computer Systems.* Santa Cruz, Calif.: Mitchell Publishing, 1987

Lenning, O. T. *Previous Attempts to Structure Educational Outcomes and Outcome-Related Concepts: A Compilation and Review of the Literature.* Boulder, Colo.: National Center for Higher Education Management Systems, 1977.

Lenning, O. T. "Assessment and Evaluation." In U. Delworth, G. R. Hanson, and Associates, *Student Services: A Handbook for the Profession.* San Francisco: Jossey-Bass, 1980.

Levine, A., and Associates. *Shaping Higher Education's Future: Demographic Realities and Opportunities, 1990–2000.* San Francisco: Jossey-Bass, 1989.

Lewis, D. R. "Costs and Benefits of Assessment: A Paradigm." In T. W. Banta (ed.), *Implementing Outcomes Assessment: Promise and Perils.* New Directions for Institutional Research, no. 59. San Francisco: Jossey-Bass, 1988.

Light, R. J., Singer, J. D., and Willett, J. B. *By Design: Planning Research on Higher Education.* Cambridge, Mass.: Harvard University Press, 1990.

Likert, R. "A Technique for the Measurement of Attitudes." *Archives of Psychology,* 1932, *140,* 44–53.

Linn, R. L. "Issues of Validity for Criterion-Referenced Measures." *Applied Psychological Measurement,* 1980, *4,* 547–561.

Linn, R. L., and Slinde, J. A. "The Determination of the Significance of Change Between Pre- and Posttesting Periods." *Review of Educational Research,* 1977, *47,* 121–150.

Loacker, G., Cromwell, L., and O'Brien, K. "Assessment in Higher Education: To Serve the Learner." In C. Adelman (ed.), *Assessment in Higher Education: Issues and Contexts.* Report no. OR 86-301. Washington, D.C.: U.S. Department of Education, 1986.

Loevinger, J. *Ego Development: Conceptions and Theories.* San Francisco: Jossey-Bass, 1976.

Mable, P. "Student Performance Assessment: The Student Affairs Obligation." *NASPA Region III Review,* Fall 1988, pp. 1–2.

McClain, C. J., and Krueger, D. W. "Using Outcomes Assessment:

A Case Study in Institutional Change." In P. T. Ewell (ed.), *Assessing Educational Outcomes.* New Directions for Institutional Research, no. 47. San Francisco: Jossey-Bass, 1985.

McMahon, E. M. "The Why, What, and Who of Assessment: The State Perspective." In *Assessing the Outcomes of Higher Education.* Proceedings of the 1986 ETS Invitational Conference. Princeton, N.J.: Educational Testing Service, 1987.

Mager, R. F. *Preparing Instructional Objectives.* Belmont, Calif.: Fearon-Pitman, 1962.

Magnarella, P. J. "The University of Vermont's Living-Learning Center: A First-Year Appraisal." *Journal of College Student Personnel,* 1975, *16,* 16–20.

Maloney, M. P., and Ward, M. P. *Psychological Assessment: A Conceptual Approach.* New York: Oxford University Press, 1976.

Marchese, T. "Learning About Assessment." *AAHE Bulletin,* 1985, *38,* 10–13.

Marchese, T. "Third Down, Ten Years to Go." *AAHE Bulletin,* 1987, *40,* 3–8.

Martenza, V. R. *Applying Norm-Referenced and Criterion-Referenced Measurement in Education.* Newton, Mass.: Allyn & Bacon, 1977.

Mayer, R. "Learning." In H. E. Mitzel, J. H. Best, and W. Rabinowitz (eds.), *Encyclopedia of Educational Research.* Vol 2, pp. 1040–1058. New York: Free Press, 1982.

Mendenhall, W., Ott, L., and Scheaffer, R. L. *Elementary Survey Sampling.* Belmont, Calif.: Wadsworth, 1971.

Mentkowski, M. "Paths to Integrity: Educating for Personal Growth and Professional Performance." In S. Srivastva and Associates, *Executive Integrity: The Search for High Human Values in Organizational Life.* San Francisco: Jossey-Bass, 1988.

Mentkowski, M., and Doherty, A. "Abilities That Last a Lifetime: Outcomes of the Alverno Experience." *AAHE Bulletin,* 1984, *37,* 8–14.

Mentkowski, M., and Loacker, G. "Assessing and Validating the Outcomes of College." In P. T. Ewell (ed.), *Assessing Educational Outcomes.* New Directions for Institutional Research, no. 47. San Francisco: Jossey-Bass, 1985.

Merton, R., Fiske, M., and Kendall, P. L. *The Focused Interview.* New York: Free Press, 1956.

Messick, S. "The Test Validation and the Ethics of Assessment." *American Psychologist,* 1980, *35,* 1012–1027.

Messick, S. "Meaning and Values in Test Validation: The Science and Ethics of Assessment." *Educational Researcher,* 1989, *18,* 5–11.

Micek, S. S., and Arney, W. R. *Inventory of Institutional Environment Variables and Measures.* Boulder, Colo.: National Center for Higher Education Management Systems, 1974.

Microsoft Corporation. *Microsoft Chart.* Bellevue, Wash.: Microsoft, 1985.

Mikulas, W. L. *Concepts in Learning.* Philadelphia: Saunders, 1974.

Miller, H. G., Williams, R. G., and Haladyna, T. M. *Beyond Facts: Objective Ways to Measure Thinking.* Englewood Cliffs, N.J.: Educational Technology Publications, 1978.

Miller, M. "Characteristics of Effective and Ineffective Assessment Programs." Keynote address at the Virginia Assessment Conference, Arlington, Dec. 1989.

Miller, P. M., and Wilson, M. J. *A Dictionary of Social Science Methods.* New York: Wiley, 1983.

Millman, J. "Passing Scores and Test Lengths for Criterion-Referenced Tests." *Review of Educational Research,* 1973, *43,* 205–216.

Millman, J. "Criterion-Referenced Measurement." In W. J. Popham (ed.), *Evaluation in Education: Current Applications.* Berkeley, Calif.: McCutchan, 1974.

Mines, R. A. "Student Development Assessment Techniques." In G. R. Hanson (ed.), *Measuring Student Development.* New Directions for Student Services, no. 20. San Francisco: Jossey-Bass, 1982.

Mitchell, M., and Jolley, J. *Research Design Explained.* New York: Holt, Rinehart & Winston, 1988.

Moos, R. H. *Evaluating Educational Environments: Procedures, Measures, Findings, and Policy Implications.* San Francisco: Jossey-Bass, 1979.

Morris, L. L., Fitz-Gibbon, C. T., and Freeman, M. F. *How to*

Communicate Evaluation Findings. Newbury Park, Calif.: Sage, 1987.

Morris, L. L., Fitz-Gibbon, C. T., and Lindheim, E. *How to Measure Performance and Use Tests.* Newbury Park, Calif.: Sage, 1987.

Murphy, R. T. "Assessment." In S. B. Anderson and others (eds.), *Encyclopedia of Educational Evaluation: Concepts and Techniques for Evaluating Education and Training Programs.* San Francisco: Jossey-Bass, 1975.

Murray, H. A. *Explorations in Personality.* Cambridge, Mass.: Harvard University Press, 1938.

Myers, S. *Every Employee a Manager.* New York: McGraw-Hill, 1970.

Nay, M. A., and Crocker, R. K. "Science Teaching and the Affective Attributes of Scientists." *Science Education,* 1970, *54,* 59–67.

Nedelsky, L. "Absolute Grading Standards for Objective Tests." *Educational and Psychological Measurement,* 1954, *14,* 3–19.

Newman, D. L., Brown, R. D., and Littman, M. "Evaluator and Audience Characteristics Which Influence the Impact of Evaluation Reports: Does Who Say What to Whom Make a Difference?" *CEDR Quarterly,* 1979, *12,* 14–18.

Novick, M. R., and Lewis, C. "Prescribing Test Length for Criterion-Reference Measurement." In C. W. Harris, M. C. Alkin, and W. J. Popham (eds.), *Problems in Criterion-Reference Measurement.* SDE Monograph Series in Evaluation, no. 3. Los Angeles: Center for the Study of Evaluation, University of California, 1974.

Oerter, R. "Development." In J. J. Eysenck, W. Arnold, and W. Meili (eds.), *Encyclopedia of Psychology.* Vol. 1. New York: Herder & Herder, 1972.

Oetting, E. R., and Cole, C. W. "Method, Design, and Implementation in Evaluation." In G. R. Hanson (ed.), *Evaluating Program Effectiveness.* New Directions for Student Services, no. 1. San Francisco: Jossey-Bass, 1978.

O'Leary, K. D., and Johnson, S. B. "Psychological Assessment." In H. C. Quay and J. S. Werry (eds.), *Psychopathological Disorders of Children.* New York: Wiley, 1979.

O'Meara, W. "Assessment of Liberal Studies Courses in Philosophy/Religion/Values." Presentation at the Fourth Annual Vag/Schen Conference on Student Assessment, Virginia Beach, Va., 1990.

Ory, J. C. "Evaluation and Assessment for Higher Education Decision Making." Paper presented at annual meeting of the American Educational Research Association, New Orleans, April 1988.

Osborne, G. M. "Report Length: A Factor Influencing Audience Perceptions of an Evaluation Study." *Educational Evaluation and Policy Analysis,* 1986, *8* (2), 205–213.

Osgood, C. E., Suci, C. J., and Tannenbaum, P. H. *The Measurement of Meaning.* Urbana: University of Illinois Press, 1957.

Osterlind, S. J. *College BASE: Guide to Test Content.* Chicago: Riverside Publishing, 1989.

Pascarella, E. T. "Are Value-Added Analyses Valuable?" In *Assessing the Outcomes of Higher Education.* Proceedings of the 1986 ETS Invitational Conference. Princeton, N.J.: Educational Testing Service, 1987a.

Pascarella, E. T. "Some Methodological and Analytic Issues in Assessing the Influence of College." Paper presented at the joint meetings of the American College Personnel Association and the National Association of Student Personnel Administrators, Chicago, 1987b.

Pascarella, E. T., and Terenzini, P. T. *Does College Make a Difference: A Review of Twenty Years of Research.* San Francisco: Jossey-Bass, 1991.

Paskow, J. (ed.). *Assessment Programs and Projects: A Directory.* Washington, D.C.: American Association for Higher Education, 1988.

Passon, A. H. "Reporting the Results of Evaluation Studies." *International Journal of Educational Research,* 1987, *2,* 115–123.

Patton, M. Q. *How to Use Qualitative Methods in Evaluation.* Newbury, Park, Calif.: Sage, 1987.

Pearson, R. "The Test Fails as an Entrance Examination." In *Should the General Composition Test Be Continued?* Special issue of *College Board Review,* 1985, *25,* 2–9.

Perry, W. G., Jr. *Forms of Intellectual and Ethical Development in the College Years.* New York: Holt, Rinehart & Winston, 1970.

Pike, G. "Review of Assessment Instruments." In C. Adelman (ed.), *Performance and Judgment.* Washington, D.C.: Office of Educational Research and Improvement, U.S. Department of Education, 1988.

Pollio, H. R., and Humphreys, W. L. "Grading Students." In J. H. McMillan (ed.), *Assessing Students' Learning.* New Directions for Teaching and Learning, no. 34. San Francisco: Jossey-Bass, 1988.

Popham, W. J. *Criterion-Referenced Measurement.* Englewood Cliffs, N.J.: Prentice-Hall, 1978.

Priestley, M. *Performance Assessment in Education and Training: Alternative Techniques.* Englewood Cliffs, N.J.: Educational Technology Publications, 1982.

Rea, P. J. "The Assessment Center as a Career Planning Tool." *Journal of Career Planning and Employment,* Spring 1987, *47,* 21–22.

Resnick, D. P. "History of Educational Testing." In A. Wigdor and W. Garner (eds.), *Ability Testing: Uses, Consequences, and Controversies.* Part 2. Washington, D.C.: National Research Council, 1982.

Resnick, D. P. "Expansion, Quality, and Testing in American Education." In D. Bray and M. J. Belcher (eds.), *Issues in Student Assessment.* New Directions for Community Colleges, no. 59. San Francisco: Jossey-Bass, 1987.

Resnick, D. P., and Goulden, M. "Assessment, Curriculum, and Expansion: A Historical Perspective." In D. F. Halpern (ed.), *Student Outcomes Assessment: What Institutions Stand to Gain.* New Directions For Higher Education, no. 59. San Francisco: Jossey-Bass, 1987.

Rest, J. *Guide for the Defining Issues Test.* Minneapolis: Center for the Study of Ethical Development, 1987.

Riecken, H. W., and Boruch, R. F. (eds.). *Social Experimentation: A Method for Planning and Evaluating Social Intervention.* San Diego, Calif.: Academic Press, 1974.

Riley, M. W., and Stoll, C. S. "Content Analysis." In D. L. Sills (ed.), *International Encyclopedia of the Social Sciences.* Vol. 3. New York: Macmillan, 1968.

Rippey, R. "Assessing Awareness of the Need to Know." Paper

presented at meeting of the American Educational Research Association, New Orleans, 1988.

Robertson, G. J. (ed.). "Classic Measurement Reference Work Revised: An Interview with Editor Robert L. Linn." *The Score,* 1989, *1.*

Robinson, J. P., and Shaver, P. R. *Measures of Social Psychological Attitudes.* Ann Arbor: Survey Research Center, Institute of Social Research, University of Michigan, 1973.

Rodgers, R. F. "An Integration of Campus Ecology and Student Development: The Olentangy Project." In D. G. Creamer and Associates (eds.), *Student Development in Higher Education: Theory and Assessment.* Vol. 2. Arlington, Va.: American College Personnel Association Media, 1990.

Roid, G. H. "The Technology of Test-Item Writing." In H. F. O'Neil (ed.), *Procedures for Institutional Systems Development.* San Diego, Calif.: Academic Press, 1979.

Roid, G. H., and Haladyna, T. M. *A Technology for Test-Item Writing.* San Diego, Calif.: Academic Press, 1982.

Rossi, P. H., Wright, J. D., and Anderson, A. B. *Handbook of Survey Research.* San Diego, Calif.: Academic Press, 1983.

Rossmann, J. E., and El-Khawas, E. *Thinking About Assessment: Perspectives for Presidents and Chief Academic Officers.* Washington, D.C.: American Council on Education and American Association for Higher Education, 1987.

Runyan, S., and Krivsky, K. "Assessment of Undergraduate Student Learning: Pilot Procedures for Speech Pathology." Paper presented at annual meeting of the American Speech-Language-Hearing Association, Boston, 1988.

Salvia, J., and Ysseldyke, J. E. *Assessment in Special and Remedial Education.* Boston: Houghton Mifflin, 1978.

SAS Institute. *SAS Procedures Guide. Version 5 Edition.* Cary, N.C.: SAS Institute, 1990.

Schermerhorn, G. R., and Williams, R. G. "An Empirical Comparison of Responsive and Preordained Approaches to Program Evaluation." *Educational Evaluation and Policy Analysis,* 1979, *1* (3), 55–60.

Shepard, L. A. "Standard Setting Issues and Methods." *Applied Psychological Measurement,* 1980, *4,* 447–465.

Shulman, L. S. "Assessment for Teaching: An Initiative for the Profession." *Phi Beta Kappan,* 1987, *69* (1), 38–44.

Slaughter, S. "From Serving Students to Serving the Economy: Changing Expectations of Faculty Role Performance." *Higher Education,* 1985, pp. 41–56.

Smode, A. F., Gruber, A., and Ely, J. H. *The Measurement of Advanced Flight Vehicle Crew Proficiency in Synthetic Ground Environments.* Report MRL-TDR-62-2. Wright-Patterson Air Force Base, Ohio: Aerospace Medical Division, 1962.

Software Publishing Corporation. *Harvard Graphics.* Mountain View, Calif.: Software Publishing Corporation, 1988.

Southern Regional Education Board, Commission for Educational Quality. *Access to Quality Undergraduate Education.* Reprinted in *Chronicle of Higher Education,* July 3, 1985, pp. 9–12.

SPSS, Inc. *Statistical Package for the Social Sciences, Version X: User's Guide.* Chicago: SPSS, Inc., 1986.

Stiggins, R. J. "NCME Instructional Yearbook: Design and Development of Performance Instruments." *Educational Measurement,* 1987, *6,* 33–42.

Strom, R. D., Bernard H. W., and Strom, S. K. *Human Development and Learning.* New York: Human Sciences Press, 1987.

Study Group on the Conditions of Excellence in American Higher Education, National Institute of Education. *Involvement in Learning: Realizing the Potential of American Higher Education.* Washington, D.C.: U.S. Government Printing Office, 1984.

Stufflebeam, D. L. "An Introduction to the PDK Book." In B. Worthen and J. R. Sanders (eds.), *Education Evaluation: Theory and Practice.* Belmont, Calif.: Wadsworth, 1973.

Stufflebeam, D. L., and others. *Educational Evaluation and Decision-Making.* Itasca, Ill.: Peacock, 1971.

Taylor, G. R., and Erwin, T. D. "A Model for Undergraduate Physics Major Outcomes Objectives." *American Journal of Physics,* 1989, *57,* 547–548.

TenBrink, T. D. *Evaluation: A Practical Guide for Teachers.* New York: McGraw-Hill, 1974.

Tennessee Higher Education Commission. *Instructional Evaluation Variables.* Nashville: Tennessee Higher Education Commission, 1983.

Thompson, P. A., Brown, R. D., and Furgason, J. "Jargon and Data Do Make a Difference: The Impact of Report Styles on Lay and Professional Evaluation Audiences." *Evaluation Review*, 1981, *5*, 269–279.

Thorndike, R. L., and Hagen, E. *Measurement and Evaluation in Psychology and Education*. New York: Wiley, 1969.

Thornton, G. C., and Byham, W. C. *Assessment Centers and Managerial Performance*. San Diego, Calif.: Academic Press, 1982.

Traub, R. E., and Wolf, R. G., "Latent-Trait Theories and Assessment of Educational Achievement." In D. C. Berliner (ed.), *Review of Research in Education 9*. Washington, D.C.: American Educational Research Association, 1981.

Trent, J. W., and Medsker, L. L. *Beyond High School: A Study of 10,000 High School Graduates*. Berkeley: Center for Research and Development in Higher Education, University of California, 1967.

Tyler, R. W. *Basic Principles of Curriculum and Instruction*. Chicago: University of Chicago Press, 1950.

U.S. Department of Education. "Secretary's Procedures and Criteria for Recognition of Accrediting Agencies." *Federal Register*, 1988, *53* (127), 25088–25099.

Vernon, P. E., and Millican, G. D. "A Further Study of the Reliability of English Essays." *British Journal of Statistical Psychology*, 1954, *7*, 65–74.

Virginia Commonwealth University. "Values." Unpublished report of the VCU Ad Hoc Value Committee, Office of Vice President for Academic Affairs, Virginia Commonwealth University, 1988.

Vobejda, B. "Evidence of Learning Sought: Bennett Moves to Make Colleges Document Student Achievement." *Washington Post*, Sept. 6, 1987, p. A8.

Warren, J. "A Model for Assessing Undergraduate Learning in Mechanical Engineering." In C. Adelman (ed.), *Signs and Traces*. Washington, D.C.: U.S. Government Printing Office, 1989.

Weaver, W. "The New Curriculum at the University of Wisconsin." In W. Gray (ed.), *Recent Trends in American College Education:*

Proceedings of the Institute for Administrative Officers of Higher Institutions. Chicago: University of Chicago Press, 1931.

Webb, E. J., Campbell, D. T., Schwartz, R. D., and Sechrest, L. *Unobtrusive Measures: Nonreactive Research in the Social Sciences.* Skokie, Ill.: Rand McNally, 1966.

Weiss, C. H. *Evaluation Research: Methods for Assessing Program Effectiveness.* Englewood Cliffs, N.J.: Prentice-Hall, 1972.

Weiss, C. H. "Research for Policy's Sake: The Enlightenment Function of Social Research." *Policy Analysis,* 1977, *3,* 531-545.

Weiss, C. H. "Measuring the Use of Evaluation." In J. A. Ciarlo (ed.), *Utilizing Evaluation: Concepts and Measurement Techniques.* Newbury Park, Calif.: Sage, 1981.

Weiss, C. H. "Where Politics and Evaluation Research Meet." *Evaluation,* 1973, *3,* 337-345.

Wergin, J. F. "The Evaluation of Organizational Policy Making: A Political Model." *Review of Educational Research,* 1976, *46* (1), 75-115.

Wergin, J. F. "Politics and Assessment in the University." In T. W. Banta (ed.), *Assessment Update: Progress, Trends, and Practices in Higher Education,* no. 2. San Francisco: Jossey-Bass, 1989.

Wesman, A. G. "Writing the Test Item." In R. L. Thorndike (ed.), *Educational Measurement.* Washington, D.C.: American Council on Education, 1971.

Whitman, R. F., and Foster, T. J. *Speaking in Public.* New York: Macmillan, 1987.

Whitney, D. R. *Improving Essay Examinations: I. Writing Essay Questions.* Technical Bulletin no. 9. Iowa City: Evaluation and Examination Service, University of Iowa, 1970.

Williams, J. R., Tiller, M. G., Herring, H. C., III, and Scheiner, J. H. *A Framework for the Development of Accounting Education Research.* Sarasota, Fla.; Coopees & Lybran Foundation and American Accounting Association, 1988.

Windle, C. and Ochberg, F. M. "Enhancing Program Evaluation in the Community Mental Health Centers Program." *Evaluation,* 1975, *2,* 30-36.

Winston, R. B., Jr., and Miller, T. K. *Student Development Task and Lifestyle Inventory Manual.* Athens, Ga.: Student Development Associates, 1987.

Wolf, R. M. *Evaluation in Education: Foundations of Competency Assessment and Program Review.* New York: Praeger, 1987.

Zieky, M. J., and Livingston, S. A. *Manual for Setting Standards on the Basic Skills Assessment Tests.* Princeton, N.J.: Educational Testing Service, 1977.

INDEX

75
_____

143
149